THIRD CULTURE KIDS
OF THE WORLD

THIRD CULTURE KIDS OF THE WORLD

EXPLORING SUSTAINABLE TRAVEL MINDSETS

PRIYANKA SURIO

NEW DEGREE PRESS

THIRD CULTURE KIDS OF THE WORLD
Exploring Sustainable Travel Mindsets

ISBN   978-1-63676-619-5 *Paperback*
             978-1-63676-294-4 *Kindle Ebook*
             978-1-63676-295-1 *Ebook*

To God.

To my ancestors and family from India and Hungary.

To my grandparents, Napa—Rev. Zoltan Kiraly and Nagymami—Susan Kiraly, who gifted me with a legacy of stories.

To all the third culture kids of the world.

CONTENTS

Let our hyphenated identities serve as the bridges of humankind. For ours will be a great generation leaving no one behind.

—PRIYANKA SURIO, INDIAN-HUNGARIAN-AMERICAN

INTRODUCTION: GLOBAL ROOTS OF OUR TIME

PARTICIPATING IN THE LARGEST GLOBAL CIVIL RIGHTS MOVEMENT OF OUR TIME

Another unarmed Black man was killed.

This time the deadly weapon was an officer's knee on a neck as he choked the life out of George Floyd using his body. And all this during the largest and most devastating global pandemic of our time.

Enough was enough. I was fired up to do something about it, both here in America and anywhere where such hatred and racism still existed in the world.

Bitter memories came rushing in as I recalled what happened to Trayvon Martin, who was only seventeen when fatally shot in Sanford, Florida, an hour and a half away from my hometown of Mulberry, Florida.

I looked out over an idyllic view of Washington, DC, from my apartment window on my way to peacefully protest on behalf of these Black lives lost too soon. I thought about how five months before George Floyd died, I was sitting in a luxurious, back alley speakeasy in Minneapolis not too far from where the act occurred. I was at the tail end of a business trip talking to locals about the influence of African Americans on Minnesota's music scene during the Jazz Age of the 1920s, while sipping on expertly crafted cocktails with the golden glow of candlelight emanating from a chandelier in the middle of the room. As I reflected on how close to home all of this felt, the fire of my rage fueled and motivated me to do more in the fight against racism.

It was time to turn the volume all the way up on the message of equality and justice for Black lives. In the words of hip-hop pioneer KRS-One, which stands for Knowledge Reigns Supreme Over Nearly Everyone, "It seems like racism in the United States is overflowing."[1]

Listening to KRS-One's iconic hit "Sound of Da Police," I looked out over the flowing water of the Potomac River as I ran the Mt. Vernon Trail toward downtown Washington, DC, unaware of what awaited next. As I approached Lafayette Square Park in front of the White House, I felt the hot anticipation in my flushed cheeks. Before I could clearly see the protestors lined up in front of an army of law enforcement, I heard them chanting above the summer heat, calling for #JusticeforGeorgeFloyd and #BlackLivesMatter. I didn't

1   Deena Zaru, "KRS-One gets political: What's fake and what's real in politics?" CNN Politics, August 16, 2017.

know it at the time, but I was standing right in the heart of what would later be called Black Lives Matter Plaza as what unfolded played out like every nightmare and horror I've seen on the media about police brutality and rioting this past year.

A cloudy haze of smoke permeated every space, except it wasn't just smoke; it was tear gas, and I was suffocating in my mask just like the young teenagers and twenty-somethings around me, coughing, retching, and gasping for air. I tried to remove my mask, but somehow that seemed to make it worse, so I put it back on and pulled my NASA hoodie over my head as I looked down at the thick rubber boots of the military police, secret service, Department of Homeland Security, and other uniformed officers blocking the entrance to the park. As I and several other protestors looked up, we were met with pepper spray, and several protestors started running back to flush their eyes with the milk that one of the protestors had brought with her.

"This is what they want," I thought, "for us to stand down and run away."

Just as I was able to blink my eyes open again, two White men in the back wearing all black started hurling something toward the officers, and before I could see what it was, another wave of gas and a loud sonic boom followed by sirens echoed down the street.

You might, at this point, be asking yourself, I thought this book was about traveling, so why start with a story about activism for a movement created by and for Black people to achieve equality and justice?

As a traveler of the world, I've come to embrace all people and cultures. I have also found that the reality of the human experience is far from a world of equality and love. This is especially true for the most marginalized people, whether it be their African heritage, the darker color of their skin, or their "otherness." As a first-generation Indian-Hungarian-American, I start with my home country and bear witness to the injustices that Black and Indigenous people have faced since the beginning of our history. For me, this injustice represents the heart of the problem and the core of what #BlackLivesMatter aims to solve. #BLM is a civil and human rights movement advocating for a world where we value the lives of people who suffer from a long history of racism and oppression. Sadly, we are not past these sins even in today's world.

We can't achieve a world where all lives matter if we can't address the original sin we've committed to darker-skinned people over thousands of years and miles.

Back at the White House, my ears rang from the cacophony of noises from bullhorns, protestors' chants and screams, sirens, car alarms, and flash-bang grenades. We tried to remain steady in our posts as police officers ordered and then forced us to clear out. I had come to the protest with a Bible in hand to pray for these officers, for my Black brothers and sisters, and for the situation that had drawn me to the front lines. I could sense things could and would escalate. If any part of me sensed I should leave, it was overwhelmed by the part of me that felt an immense empathy; I wanted to make sure the protestors were safe and supported, an act that came with personal risks. It meant breaking social distancing rules for COVID-19 to link arms with fellow protestors as they stood their ground to the officers. These youth had shown up at the protest, ready and willing to fight for this cause like their lives depended on it. To be a true ally and prioritize their lives like I said I did, I had to be equally willing to fight for this cause. Emboldened and inspired by the hurt, bravery, and rage in their eyes, I decided to stand with them in their convictions.

To arrive at this difficult decision, I reflected upon my own experiences with racism and conjured up my own hurt, bravery, and rage. Hurt, as a little girl who experienced racism while growing up in central Florida. Bravery, as a teenager traveling to DC with an earnest yearning for change. Rage, as a recent college grad relocating to DC to build a career, determined to make a difference.

The moments we were able to demonstrate solidarity were beautiful because even though we'd never met each other before and were from different walks of life, we hugged each other, supported one another, linked arms in a line to face the police together, and sat down in meditation to show we weren't a threat. That night, and the protest days after, were examples of anti-racist activism, which brought about a strong sense of community and love for my fellow brethren.

In the coming days, our impact from that night and others showed itself by instigating protests in all fifty states and across the world in eighteen plus countries.[2]

Beyond that, Mayor Bowser of DC changed the name of the street leading to Lafayette Square Park to Black Lives Matter Plaza and commissioned a painting of the words "Black Lives Matter" along that road.[3] Feeling more like damage control, we protesters knew the work was far from over.

TRAVELING AS A GLOBAL ACTIVIST

Starting off 2020 in the midst of two global pandemics, one spreading biologically through a novel coronavirus (COVID-19) and the other a social pandemic of racism, changed my perspective on why I travel. I decided any future traveling would be planned in such a way to prioritize and value the lives of Black and Indigenous people of color. I had already traveled extensively for what I considered solid reasons:

- exploring my roots by visiting my parents' home countries
- studying abroad
- volunteering abroad
- backpacking
- practicing or learning another language

---

2   Larry Buchanan, Quoctrung Bui, and Jugal K. Patel, "Black Lives Matter May Be the Largest Movement in US History," New York Times, July 3, 2020.

3   "Mayor Bowser Renames a Portion of 16th Street, NW to Black Lives Matter Plaza," Office of the Mayor, Government of the District of Colombia, accessed June 9, 2020.

- witnessing climate change firsthand
- building resilience through solo traveling

With COVID-19 halting travel for many of us, there was nowhere to go and only time to dream about the places we longed to visit. During that time, I reflected on each of my past travel experiences. I realized that I personally wanted to travel with a purpose, rooted in activism wherever possible, so I could continue to amplify the causes I support on a global scale. While I was working on this book, I found myself reaching out to people all around the world, starting with where I grew up in Polk County and extending to friends I had made on my travels abroad in the name of collaborating for a more equal and sustainable world. As soon as my first few collaborations were complete, I knew this way of traveling and collaborating with friends and communities would make up a substantial part of my future travels.

TOURISM'S OXYMORON

Many tourists I've met on the road speak to what they can get from the experience of travel, which is often influenced by a consumer-driven mentality. Others may envision the ideal dream vacation on a beach sipping cocktails or taking the perfect picture on a mountaintop to generate the most likes on social media. Still, others don't understand how to be responsible, sustainable, or culturally sensitive on their trips, even though they may have heard about it and are interested in doing so. There are two moments where I witnessed tourists' sense of entitlement on my trips. I had booked what I thought were English-speaking tours to see Tayrona National Park in Colombia and the forested mountains amid the rivers of Guilin, China. I ended up with tour guides who spoke in their native language. I could visibly see the frustration of the English speakers around me—as I'm sure the tour guide could—as they sighed, rolled their eyes, or started complaining to one another about the inaccurate marketing of the tour and how that would reflect in their review. I could understand their frustration; they wished to learn about the culture, which was difficult to do when they didn't understand what was being communicated.

One way to experience culture is through the people we interact with, and if our only interactions are those of distaste and frustration, this is the message we are communicating to those locals who spend their time showing us their homeland. In my experience, I find it beautiful to listen to people speak in their native tongue, which also motivates me to learn phrases or common words when visiting a new country where the locals speak other languages besides English. When I take the time to learn a few phrases, locals are immensely happy to hear my attempts at communicating in their language and often willing to be my language teacher for the hour, day, week, or month.

On the one hand, the tourism industry has grown the airline industry into what it is today and subsequently enhanced the service industry. Nonetheless, as aviation increased, it made me wonder about the darker side of this growth, such as the amount of carbon emissions released into the atmosphere. The International Air Transport Association (IATA), which represents the interests of most of the world's airline companies, outlined this growth in their recent contribution to the 2019 Aviation Benefits report. In 2018, airlines carried

4.3 billion passengers on nearly 50,000 routes worldwide, covering fifty-four billion kilometers.[4] That's a lot of people covering quite the distance. Given present trends, IATA predicts passenger numbers could double to 8.2 billion by 2037.[5]

But as people travel to and spend their dollars in other places, there are opportunities to strengthen our connections as a human race through responsible tourism. Tourism fuels local businesses and, in some cases, brings back a resurgence of culture and community to places that were previously dying out or dangerous. Tourism also provides opportunities for us to explore what we like about new places through walking tours, historical places, food, and cultural experiences, and more recently, the use of social media to incite wanderlust as a travel influencer or digital nomad.

EXPLORING SUSTAINABILITY

So, is it wrong to fly? When exploring that question, I looked to several private industry companies in the tourism, aviation, and hospitality space. I found out that for the past few decades, a lot of research has gone into exploring the possibility of electric flights or flying on hydrogen fuel. The reality is this option remains extremely difficult and expensive, unable to keep up with the demands of the aviation industry. Current electric planes can only fit a few people at a time over a short distance. The fact that it will take several more decades until this is a reality puts the responsibility back on us as the traveler to be more committed to figuring out

---

4   2019 Aviation Benefits Report, Industry High-level Group (2020).

5   Ibid.

a solution for carbon offsets before we book that next flight, or to at the least, have an intentional purpose behind why we need to and should travel to a place. As I began contemplating my own modes of transportation across the globe and reflecting on my sustainability toward the environment, I also remembered a conversation I had with my mother about how sustainable my lifestyle of near constant traveling was.

"Another trip? . . . I can't keep up," my mother said.

"Yes," I sighed.

She was right. It had been a flurry of travel as my latest work trip to South Carolina was my third this month. Even I couldn't keep up with it. What started out as exciting was soon becoming exhausting from being in and out of planes, cars, and strange homes that were not my own. I am a self-proclaimed nature lover, but could I really call myself an environmentalist given all the flights and road trips I had taken? Beyond that, the guilt started setting in, reminding me of how the evening fog of San Francisco blankets everything in its path, sometimes not even sparing the Golden Gate. I asked myself, what if our carbon emissions escalated to the point where it blanketed the Earth like this fog, and we couldn't see any of our planet's beauty? When I think about how we as humans have been treating each other and the planet for centuries, perhaps we don't deserve that privilege.

Nonetheless, traveling to other places at home and across the world has made me a better person by opening my mind to other cultures and ways of life, teaching me resilience and adaptability resulting in my personal and professional successes, and connecting me with my family's ethnic heritage when visiting them abroad. In my search to strike a balance between these various conflicts inherent in my own traveling experience, I reflected on what mindsets, when applied intentionally, could achieve both reduced carbon emissions and responsible engagement with other cultures.

I hear the skeptics asking whether their small actions will really make a difference toward achieving sustainability in an increasingly globalized world, connected even more by the travel industry. Based on my research, interviews, and experiences, the answer is yes. In that discovery of the truth, I have uncovered a more intentional way to think about traveling to include reflecting on what you leave behind. I've set out on a personal journey to explore ways we can still continue traveling while not increasing our negative impacts on other cultures, the environment, or local economies. In short, my journey has required more time and effort to find the truth as I come to understand what I love about traveling and my respective impact on the people I've met along the way.

I reflected on everything I've learned around the world as I've traveled. I knew I wanted to share what I had learned with others, so I created a simple formula for sustainable travel that would show us how we can use traveling to make the world a better place for all of us.

There are essentially four mindsets in my sustainable travel formula, which can lead to four world-changing forces, none completely novel and probably something you've heard before in various contexts. Nonetheless, we'll explore each of these in the context of how they can be applied when you are on your travels at home or abroad.

The mindsets were created to inspire better travel and inspire a commitment to global citizenry. As such, the first chapter explains how to navigate the contents of this book based on how you identify as a traveler. You may be starting out on your travel journey and, therefore, interested in learning the best way to visit or live in another place. You may consider yourself a more seasoned traveler who envisions a life, career, or experiences that know no borders. Or maybe you choose to live vicariously through the travelers and nomads of the world because you enjoy learning, watching, reading, or listening to people who have traveled afar from the comforts of your home.

I also decided to write a book about sustainable travel because, as I looked around at prominent travel influencers, I realized the number of Black and Brown travel influencers was minimal, and the challenges we personally faced as people of color navigating the world, were not prominently featured by the industry. To change this trend, my book features the perspectives and travel stories of Africans, darker-skinned people, third culture kids (TCKs), and myself. Documenting my travels has also inspired me to pave the way for other Brown travelers to step out of their comfort zone to authentically experience more of the world and share their stories.

Finally, each and every person I informally interviewed or spoke with about this book is an incredibly special part of this journey. I spoke with friends and complete strangers alike, on planes, car rides, and trains about what it means to be a better traveler.

Some of the stories featured in this book are of those who have traveled far and wide. Others may have taken regular trips across the country or ocean for work or to volunteer for causes they are passionate about. Some stories depict the lives of immigrants who were originally from other countries so vastly different from my own, working on the newest chapter of their lives in America. Some travelers have gone back to their roots by moving to their home country, and others have sought out a nomadic lifestyle of new experiences to challenge their views, add perspective, or become more well-rounded. This book can only capture a fraction of the hundreds of hours of beautiful stories I heard. If I did this again with a new group of people, I'm sure I'd have even more riches in my travel stories treasure box, and maybe I will next time I hit the road. There's a reason I chose to speak to each and every one of you, and your stories in and of themselves have been the reward.

My hope is that as you read this book, you too will learn how to be a better traveler by being more intentional, practicing the elements of the sustainable travel mindset, and doing your part in small ways to make this planet a healthier and friendlier place to thrive.

As you dive into the pages, we'll explore the mindsets needed to advance sustainable travel. The mindsets will equip us to be better global citizens as we tackle global challenges that are impacted or influenced by how we travel, such as racism and mono-culturalism, climate change, over- and under-tourism, and negative human impacts on the Earth and its creatures. The mindsets will also help us recognize that our world is becoming increasingly globalized, mixed, and filled with TCKs whose loyalties may not lie with one country alone. We'll travel "'round the world" as I share the stories of people who have exhibited aspects of each sustainable travel mindset when living in or visiting each of the continents.

A couple of stories will be my own. I have reflected on some of the most meaningful experiences I've had in America and abroad, realizing I have become quite the knowledge base for things like backpacking, camping, hosteling, road tripping, work-cations, multi-country trips, study abroad, voluntourism, female solo travel, group travel, and travel to faraway places. I want to gift you the beauty of building a life well-traveled while also ensuring we gift the people, lands, and animals we are traveling to see.

Our common human experience, our yearning for community, and the quest for happiness through connection, whether it's a person or nature itself, are the motivations I have kept in mind for each story I share. I believe we have a responsibility to make knowledge supreme so we can make an educated decision on our impact when we travel or engage other cultures.

By reading this book, you are already taking the first step of what I hope will be many along your path to building a sustainable travel mindset. I hope you'll reference what you learn here when you take a walk in the backyard, hike that mountain, drive to the other side of town, take your seat on a train across the country, board your flight, or man a boat to another land.

In the words of Patty, a humble world mountaineer and leadership training coach from Patagonia, Chile, "There's a common humanity when we [travel]. It doesn't matter if we are rich or poor, when we come to the mountain, we are the same."

PART I

PREPARING FOR YOUR JOURNEY

And perhaps the journey was never mine, could never have been mine [alone]. From the get-go, it belonged to other people.

—ROBYN DAVIDSON, INSIDE TRACKS

Before you explore and apply the sustainable travel mindsets, you'll need to understand what your journey will entail. You will define your approach to your travels. You will then need to document and measure how sustainable that is. You will ask yourself a series of questions to uncover the purpose behind your travels. You will then consider how you can use travel to change your life and the world for the better.

CHAPTER 1

HOW TO USE THIS BOOK AS A ROADMAP FOR SUSTAINABLE TRAVEL

By road, by rail, by air, and by sea, I've made my way around the world to forty countries.

As someone who identifies as a sustainable traveler, I've aimed to tread gently every step of the way, recognizing the immense privilege of traveling in the first place. I felt so good about the steps I had taken to embrace other cultures while curbing my carbon footprint that I decided to pay it forward in service to our planet: I'd write a book to teach others to do the same.

As I've traveled extensively across six continents, I've also thought about my own place in the world and about how the world might view me. Ethnically, I am a mystery to most people I encounter on my trips, as they look at me and see a Brown-skinned woman. However, this makes sharing my Indian-Hungarian-American cultures that much more rewarding.

The intersections of these cultures make me, Priyanka, a third culture kid (TCK) of this world. My journeys represent my choice to travel as a global activist, adopting sustainable travel mindsets and striving to leave each place better than when I arrived.

Becoming a responsible global citizen begins with taking responsibility for yourself and our planet. As you read through each chapter, you'll learn to ask yourself questions to help determine whether a specific type of travel experience is repeatable or sustainable, questions you'll return to every time you travel, no matter where you go.

The five-step process I outline has taught and continues to teach me about my own travel journey. As we move through the stories and exercises presented in these chapters, I'll share what I've learned and lay out a roadmap to help you navigate your own sustainable travels. Along the way, you'll discover the mindset most relevant to your own journey. Prioritize it and begin to understand it for yourself.

Now that you know who I am and the perspective I bring to this topic, I'll introduce you to the five-step process we'll implement to prepare you to explore sustainable travel mindsets.

THE FIRST STEP: CARBON FOOTPRINT CALCULATOR

First, I'd need to calculate the carbon impact of my travels. As it turns out, gathering information to perform that calculation is a complex, multi-step process, requiring meticulous documentation of my flights, connections, and ground travel. I spent much of the past four years traveling for work, taking vacations, and making time to visit with family, but had already forgotten the details surrounding my transit. But here's something I won't soon forget: My journeys across the globe over the past four years have contributed sixty metric tons of CO_2 in the air, give or take.[6]

Sixty metric tons sounds like a large number, but what does that really mean as it relates to the environment and my carbon footprint?

To better understand my footprint, I turned to the greenhouse gas equivalencies calculator, developed by the Environmental Protection Agency (EPA) and accessible through EPA.gov. I learned that the sixty metric tons of CO_2 emitted through my travel roughly equates to the volume of greenhouse gas and CO_2 emitted by:

- Thirteen individual vehicles driven for a year
- 149,000 miles driven by a vehicle in total or my car's mileage after a decade of driving

---

6   "Flight carbon footprint calculator," Carbon Footprint, accessed May 5, 2020; "Carbon Footprint Calculator," Conservation International, accessed May 5, 2020; "Carbon Calculator," TerraPass, accessed May 6, 2020; "ICAO Carbon Emissions Calculator," International Civil Aviation Organization, accessed May 6, 2020.

- Ten homes' electricity use for one year
- Seven homes' energy use for one year
- 6,751 gallons of gasoline consumed
- 66,000 pounds of coal burned
- 2,400 propane cylinders used for home barbecues—that's a lot of BBQ
- 7.6 million smartphones charged[7]

CO_2 pollution contributes to global warming. While I can't undo what I've done, there are ways to offset my contribution by implementing specific behaviors that mitigate an equivalent volume of CO_2 pollution.

In other words, I can do an equal amount of good for the atmosphere in the future to cancel out the potential harm I've contributed in the past.

In my case, to offset the CO_2 and greenhouse gas emissions I've contributed, I would need to actively prevent sixty metric tons of CO_2 that—without my intervention—would enter the environment. In the real world, that requires I rescue 2,500 trash bags of waste bound for landfills and divert the contents to recycling instead.[8] Alternatively, I could plant, nurture, and grow a thousand trees for ten years.[9]

Suddenly, with this realization, I lost my enjoyment for entertaining friends with stories of the most exotic places

---

7   "Energy and the Environment: Greenhouse Gas Equivalencies Calculator," US Environmental Protection Agency, last modified March 2020.

8   Ibid.

9   Ibid.

I've visited or comparing notes with other travelers on the number of countries I've stepped foot in. All I could think about was the enormous environmental footprint my best intentions had left behind.

THE SECOND STEP: THE WHY & WHAT

As I reflect on the numbers, I realize I'm wrestling with my conscience and the reasons why I travel in the first place. I decide to apply a concept I use in my daily work, the five whys, to get to the root cause or source of the problem.[10]

I extrapolate the whys to answer questions that would foster intentionality with the way we travel. If we can be more intentional, we can apply the sustainable travel mindsets with confidence.

- Why are you traveling this way?
- Why are you traveling here?
- Why will you do those things you've planned?
- Why do **you** specifically need or want to be here?
- Why do others need or want you to be here?

Beyond the whys, the what is equally important to consider.

- So what? What's your purpose for traveling the way you do?

---

10 "5 Whys: The Ultimate Root Cause Analysis Tool," Kanbanize, accessed May 10, 2020.

In thinking through these questions, I centered myself around the purpose of wanting to be love to those who are love to me all around the world because, in my mind, love represents the cornerstone of what it means to be a global citizen and fuels my passion for activism.

Beyond identifying my purpose for travel, I also asked myself how I would go about traveling in a way that's practical, safe, and sustainable? I borrowed a simple concept from my Indian culture—mindfulness—and repurposed it to develop a formula for mindful and sustainable travel experiences. To be more mindful, first, I had to learn the truth about our increasingly globalized world and how it came to be. Then I had to be open-minded enough to get out of my comfort zone by traveling to different places at home and abroad, including places not featured on a tourist list or ranking. After exploring new settings around the world time and again, I found I could easily overcome my fears about the place or the journey to get there. As I continued to break bread with strangers-turned-friends around the world, I thought about how I could continue to give back to local and global communities alike, inspiring a more connected world.

However, it is not enough to solely reflect on this sage traveler's wisdom, one also needs to take all these insights out on the open road, perhaps even literally, to really understand your impact.

Once I was out on the road, especially during my solo road trips around the country, I would spend time reflecting on the five whys while challenging my old habits and strengthening my mindset toward a sustainable way of traveling the world.

FOR ACTION

Write out your answers to these WHY and WHAT questions in the worksheet below. As you navigate the mindsets and topics of the book, you'll want to reference them to see where you can grow and where you are already more sustainable in your travels. I have provided my answers for inspiration.

WHYS & WHAT Worksheet

Five Whys and What	My Answer	Your answer
Why are you traveling this way?	*I like to choose the most sustainable, environmentally friendly way to reach a destination. Once there, I strive to be self-sufficient and resourceful with what I have.*	
Why are you traveling here?	*I used to keep a bucket list of places to visit. Now I plan my travel around serendipitous moments, invitations, and opportunities that align with causes and local projects I'm passionate about.*	
Why will you do those things you've planned?	*I want to leave a positive impact wherever I go and to know—at the end of every trip—I've spent time building authentic connections with the locals.*	

Why do you need or want to be here?	When I visit or return to a country, I also bring my skillsets, perspectives, and multi-ethnic cultures. One of my core interests as a traveler is to learn about the world and what it has to offer. I enjoy interacting and learning about cultures by trying local food, learning the local languages, and supporting the local economy. I want to leave a place better off than when I started, whether by recycling, or by donating my time and resources.	
Why do others need or want you to be here?	Before I plan a trip to a specific destination, I ask myself, Did locals ask or invite me to visit them? If not, then it is up to me to find out about local efforts that I can get involved with in response to the community's or country's needs.	
So what? What is your purpose?	To leave a place better than I arrived through global activism.	

If you don't have the answers to all of the five whys, that's okay, too, because not only will I equip you for the road, I'll teach you how to be a sustainable traveler.

I'm going to take you on a journey around the world through the magic sand dunes of the Merzouga Sahara Desert; the open grasslands of Mongolia; the spice-filled, packed markets of India; the rugged trek up the Chilean mountains of Patagonia; the colorful and graffitied streets of Medellin, Colombia; and the historical streets of DC during the Black

Lives Matter protests, all while keeping the ever-sunny neighborhoods of Mulberry, Florida—my hometown—in mind.

By the end of this book, I can assure you that you'll either have your answers on sustainability, or you'll be fired up to embark on or continue your travel journey no matter how near or far you intend to travel to find your answers. I'll also teach you about these places and cultures so you can understand what I learned along the way and enrich your perspective.

THE THIRD STEP: LEARN & EXPERIENCE THE WORLD
No teacher is more impactful than *firsthand experience.*

I made mistakes, and I had to fail before learning to be a more sustainable traveler. Once I started traveling the world, I learned a great deal about the uniqueness of each culture, which opened my mind to be more accepting of authentic experiences with local. I expand on these lessons in the chapters under the finding truth mindset.

My field travel experiences also taught me that the tips or stories I read about in blogs and articles aren't enough to give me a full understanding of how to engage with people and environments around the world. Not only is being a sustainable traveler a very personal journey of growth, but it also leaves an impression upon the locals you engage with, opening doors for lasting international connections. We explore these connections further in the chapters under the open-mindedness mindset.

Unlike the destinations we visit where you get to the place you are going; the sustainable travel mindset is more of an ideal to embrace when on the road. To decide to be a sustainable traveler is a journey in and of itself and a path you will continue to follow once you've chosen it for yourself. The path itself should allow for you to travel like it is second nature so that you can, without someone else's bias, understand what it means to figure out and live in a place for yourself. You will also constantly evolve and strengthen this sustainable travel mindset, the more you travel with it in mind.

When I first started traveling, I began with detailed itineraries. Eventually, I became more comfortable with knowing what type of traveler I was, what my limits were, and what things I enjoyed most about a place. I reached a point where you could drop me anywhere, and I could make it work in that country or place with minimal planning. If you'd like to understand how I accomplished that, I recommend the chapters under the open-mindedness and resilience mindsets.

Furthermore, I find beauty in discovering a place and learning from it firsthand versus reading through copious guidebooks or websites. There's this running joke in my family that every time I come back from a trip, I want to move there.

I'll say, "I absolutely loved it there. I didn't think I would love it so much, but I have to go back. Hell, maybe I'll move there."

And my brothers, mother, uncle, father, or cousins respond, "Didn't you say that about the last three places? You'll need to live an infinite lifetime at the rate you are going; there's just no way you could carry out your multiple lives in all these places."

My family is right. I don't simply want to pass through 195 named countries (193 of which are member states of the United Nations and two of which are nonmember observers and include the Holy Sea and Palestine). I want to live, work, give back, buy local, laugh, eat street food, love, explore, make friends, and fully experience each destination as comfortably as I would if I lived there. I'd love to fully experience every country in the world. If you'd like to learn about a slower pace to traveling, I recommend reading about the slow travel movement in the pursuit of happyness chapter.

Traveling to all the countries is difficult to accomplish while balancing real-life responsibilities and the pressures of a career in America's work-hard, work-fast culture. Even for those of us fortunate enough to work a fixed schedule with a fixed salary and bank of paid vacation days, extended leisure time can often remain a scarce commodity based on preexisting work cultures or expectations. For those who work in the gig economy or have non-salaried positions, time off means forgone income.

If this describes you, some of the recommended strategies may seem out of reach. The chapters within the finding truth and open-mindedness mindsets will inspire you to embrace road trips as flexible, affordable, and safer opportunities to experience new places on a near whim while remaining close to home.

Despite your unique and personal limitations or opportunities, you'll find this book a useful tool for cultivating a global perspective in an increasingly globalized world. If that's your goal, you'll particularly enjoy the chapters under the open-mindedness and giving back mindsets.

As I was writing this book, there was this one particular weekend in the middle of the COVID-19 pandemic when I had nothing else to do and nowhere else to go but climb the proverbial mountain of articles, travel stories, and self-help books I liked. While I navigated this pile of knowledge and copious information, l meditated to the soothing storytelling voice of Neil Gaiman as he ironically taught the art of storytelling.

I had all this great content at my fingertips, which was at once inspiring and overwhelming, much like how I felt when I first began to travel.

At that moment, I realized to get this right, to be a more sustainable traveler, I was doing exactly what needed to be done, which is spending more time learning about travel in all its wanderlust-filled winding paths of wondrous beauty and by documenting the journey. During this labor of love, I found myself:

- curating my own sustainable travel experiences
- talking with countless friends and fellow travelers on the road
- researching and collecting data from hundreds of sources

I feel I benefited from the pandemic if only for the amount of relatable content that travel influencers and the industry put out during the months we were on global lockdown and couldn't travel anywhere. These insights are also captured in the chapters under the resilience and giving back mindsets.

More importantly, I benefited from the valuable reflections of my own travel experiences to include what I was sharing back with the world through these trips.

THE FOURTH STEP: FIND AND LOVE YOURSELF

Some of you self-proclaimed intermediate travelers or nomads will naturally gravitate toward reading about a place I've highlighted in the book, and that's okay because perhaps you're thinking of going there yourself and you wish to understand why some of the experiences and lessons were born out of that country or state. Others will seek personal growth and wish to flip through the pages until they find the specific mindset or travel experience they yearn to strengthen or learn about when applying it to their own travels.

And yet others will be most intrigued by my own personal travel journey, which started out exploring my roots in India and Hungary through study abroad and family-sponsored trips, respectively, and quickly turned to travel as an activist in the heart of our nation's capital and in Morris County, New Jersey fighting a war on racism. I could never have imagined or planned that the DC Black Lives Matter protests would happen midway through me writing this book. Yet it brought me full circle in my travel journey because, at that point, I finally knew with genuine conviction the answer to my whys and whats.

Before I could find this out about myself, though, I literally had to figure out who I was and learn to love that person. Once I loved her, I could love others and spurn a chain reaction, an infinite amount of forward-moving love. After I learned this concept, I was able to reflect or embark on the journey of the four mindsets, some of which happened while at home discovering myself and others which were firmed up on the road before, during, and after writing this book.

I also found myself in my travels by practicing mindfulness and having a lot of honest conversations with myself about what makes me happy at home and abroad. If mindfulness is a practice you'd like to experience while on your trips, the chapter on the pursuit of happyness, within the finding truth mindset, is a journey on which you may need to embark.

A few of you might be wondering what kind of traveler you are and what that word means to you.

Perhaps you are a global activist, a travel photographer, a nomad, a hiker/camper, a backpacker, a vacationer on the road to happiness, a global entrepreneur or businesswoman/man, or a travel writer. Personally, I could see myself applying all of these as I have personified them during different moments of my journey. I look at this as more of an evolution. As you read about the sustainable travel mindsets in this book, you'll see how each of them build off one another to help you reach the goal of being a sustainable traveler and better global citizen.

I'm not here to tell you what kind of traveler you are. You'll have to come to that realization at the end of this journey, just like I have in my journey of reflection. And if my book does its job, perhaps you'll discover your own terms and purpose by the end of the last line of the last page.

THE FINAL STEP: PAY IT FORWARD

The last charge I'll give to you as a reader of this book is to either physically or mentally carry the sustainable travel mindsets with you on your travels so that you can use them as a platform to engage others about your unique travel story and share the ways in which you strive to be a better traveler. The last chapter includes a global citizen pledge, or call to action, to take with you on the road and share with others.

Who knows? If each of us just shares our story and the energy of our love with three other people, orders of magnitude show that we'll spread faster than a pandemic or racism.

That's the kind of global spread we should champion.

CHAPTER 2

A SIMPLE FORMULA FOR SUSTAINABLE TRAVEL MINDSETS

———

In thinking through my own travels and pairing that with what were widely considered sustainable travel concepts, I created a formula that I have personally reflected on and plan to incorporate more intentionally in my own travels moving forward.

What I found time and again is that, when applied, these four traits can ultimately lead us to answer yes when asked, Are we being sustainable? Do our actions make a difference?

What difference are we making exactly? To answer that, I compared my experiences and the mindsets I created with preexisting definitions for terms that various organizations in the travel industry had come up with, which includes responsible, better, smarter, ethical, regenerative, sustainable travel. If you conduct your own search of these terms, you're bound to stumble over the hundreds of variations in their definition, with some terms remaining elusive in their meaning.

When I created and reflected on each of the four mindsets, I found they lead to four world-changing forces which represent the concept of sustainable travel today. If we intentionally apply the mindsets, they can repeat and sustain long into the future, making our world a better place than where we are currently leaving it.

To bring this formula to life, this book will take you on a journey to explore exactly how and why this works through the evidence I've curated for you, the stories of real-world travelers, and my own personal experiences.

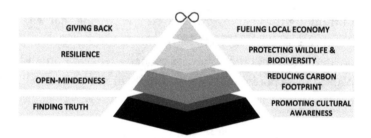

Sustainable Travel Mindsets + World-Changing Forces

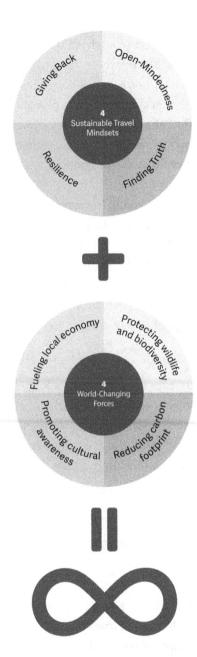

A Sustainable Travel Mindset Formula: 4 + 4 = ∞

The infinity suggests that by applying these mindsets through the formula and achieving these outcomes, we will be able to repeat and sustain our way of travel easily and responsibly without further damage to our planet, other cultures, or creatures. The infinity also signifies a future of traveling for all where we can leverage activism, technology, nomadic principles, and exploration for good.

While exploring sustainable travel mindsets, a few notable personal experiences and realizations came to the forefront. While the answers may change over time, they represent an exercise of walking through the mindset formula and should be revisited during any of your travels. You may also find that not every trip provides an opportunity to practice all the mindsets, but it may prompt you to seek that out in future trips.

Mine and others' experiences in the book should also inspire you to think of your own as you navigate and learn more about each of the mindsets. You can learn and practice these mindsets anywhere, including your own backyard. It's what you do with them and where you take them that will leave an impact on the world.

SUSTAINABLE TRAVEL MINDSETS

FINDING TRUTH

I initially learned this when I had the opportunity to visit both my parents' homelands in India and Hungary. I learned about how the caste system entrenched in India's history and the aftereffects of colonization still permeate today. I learned about how the racism against the Gypsy and Roma people in Hungary makes them feel like outsiders unable to productively contribute to their society. I also met some of my extended family for the first time, all of which taught me an immense amount about my ethnic heritage.

Once the COVID-19 global pandemic occurred and I couldn't travel anymore, I learned I had been using some of those travel experiences as a form of escaping unhappiness. I found out I had been escaping traumas experienced as a child, as a teenager, and as a twenty-something, instead of facing them head-on.

With nothing but months of time on my hands, I did the hard work of rediscovering and learning myself. At first, this was overwhelming and painful because it required me to dig deep into some of the reasons why I was escaping and what I wanted to tackle first about my life that I didn't like. I realized I had not established clear boundaries between the commitments in my life—from work to family to relationships with others. My lifestyle was a source of burnout, draining me from being the best version of myself.

Regardless of how philanthropic or environmentally friendly the trip, I realized this was unsustainable the first time I came back home after time away and found myself plotting and planning my next getaway. Once I was honest with myself, the process of building a life I wanted to come home to became easier. Many of my travel experiences were sources of inspiration for this newly created life, which infused practices from other countries to include cuisine, music, and social experiences. As I set boundaries, I found I didn't need to seek out escapes and could be more intentional on my trips moving forward.

The process of uncovering the truth also required finding love for myself. As I came to accept and love myself, I found I wanted to give that love to others amid a sometimes-scary-and-painful world.

During this same time, I also became extremely active with the antiracism protests in DC and the Black Lives Matter movement to include grassroots efforts in Morristown, New Jersey. I had always surrounded myself with the truth that permeates America's troubled origins of colonization and slavery, but this time I decided I would become even more entrenched in the cause. What I learned in that experience is that at its core, the Black Lives Matter Movement is about valuing Black lives through love and acceptance of consistently undervalued and overlooked people. We couldn't love all humanity and eliminate the forces of racism and oppression without dealing with our most marginalized periods throughout history: slavery, caste systems, colonization, genocide, apartheid, colorism, and more.

I found my calling as a global activist while spreading love through the gifts, talents, and platforms I am privileged to use for the causes I stand up for. The cause I am currently supporting is the fight against racism.

OPEN-MINDEDNESS

Four years ago, I decided to get back into international travel. My main purpose behind traveling was to better understand my place in the world as a Third Culture Kid (TCK) and to navigate the mix of cultural identities based on my ethnicity and where I grew up. I also wanted to learn as much as I could about other cultures around the world.

I explored commonly traveled places like Spain, England, France, China, Japan, and Australia.

I was equally interested in better understanding less commonly traveled places like Inner Mongolia, Ethiopia, Palestine, and the demilitarized zone (DMZ) between South and North Korea.

After the first time I traveled, I knew the best way to approach my trip was to go in with no expectations and let the experience unfold, taking in both the good and the bad. Afterward, I would reflect on the experience of the lessons I learned. With this new knowledge gained, I was able to easily befriend, work with, and support those of other cultures, backgrounds, beliefs, sexual orientations, skin colors, abilities, and languages, among other things.

I also remained open to my accommodations to include trying out Airbnb, hostels, and other shared economy services. This allowed me to get comfortable in a sharing environment while getting to know other people from around the world.

Now I look forward to striking up a conversation whether it's as whole-hearted as a cultural tour where each of us is practicing our moderate Spanish with the guide or audaciously attempting to communicate with the Yakuza at a corner food market in Kyoto, Japan by miming and using common

English words. I embraced the challenge to deepen my connections with my heritage by strengthening my language skills to develop native fluency in Hungarian and formally learning Hindi.

Being on the open road will naturally open your mind. Because I too, am different, I am able to find the beauty in what is un-American and foreign to me. I also travel with an immense amount of respect for the country and its people, demonstrated by their open borders welcoming me in.

Of course, this becomes difficult when the people you encounter harbor their own prejudices and rely on preexisting notions about what you might be like. In those instances, I found the next mindset to be helpful.

RESILIENCE

In the diversity of my travel experiences, to include six of the seven continents and places where English isn't the primary language or even spoken, I found adaptation a continual challenge. The experience of putting yourself in unfamiliar places with unfamiliar people and customs can build up your agility to roll with the punches or fruit punch that comes with life's unexpected surprises.

I traveled solo on more than half of my trips, which required a level of preparation and common sense, especially as a woman traveling. Underestimated or questioned by others about whether I could do a certain activity or travel to a certain place fueled my motivation to see for myself. Being a woman also required me to be hyper-vigilant of my surroundings and the people I engaged with or trusted. I sought trusted tours or hosts to ensure my safety and sometimes traveled with companions or family members if I felt unsafe. Nonetheless, I embrace solo traveling as one of the most empowering decisions of my life.

Camping and hiking through the rugged and raw terrains of significant mountain ranges also built up my resilience. Think Machu Picchu and Huayna Picchu (the more ominous Picchu they don't tell you about), Trolltunga in Norway, Scotland's Isle of Skye, Mongolia's Grasslands, and a desert camp in the middle of the Sahara Desert of Morocco, several US National Parks, the Colorado Great Sand Dunes Park (where I lost my tent and had to car camp), the rose golden beaches on the island of Oahu in Hawaii, and Patagonia, Chile where I pitched my first tent alone and camped for the first time in over a decade.

After tackling the outdoors in unfamiliar places, I felt like I could handle any obstacles that would come my way and achieve the dreams I set my sights on.

My latest test in resilience has been a physical, mental, and emotional challenge as I participated in a week and a half of protesting in DC, which culminated in a reunion at Malcolm X Park. I reminisced with fellow #SwannStrong protestors whom I was with when we were beaten, pepper-sprayed, and arrested on Swann Street for peacefully protesting for Black Lives Matter and justice for all the Black lives lost due to police brutality and racism across America.

While there was and still is immense trauma associated with my nights of protesting, I have grown stronger in my convictions upon seeing the immediate changes that took place after our historical experience.

GIVING BACK

I initially learned how to give back while on the streets of Mulberry in Polk County, Florida. I used to go around the neighborhood with my blue wagon collecting canned goods for a homeless shelter, Lighthouse Ministries. Since then, I've given back to countries I've visited, including India and Hungary.

During my time studying abroad in India, I donated my time to help some of the communities I visited. I volunteered at the Aksharavani school for migrant worker's children, the Save the Rock Foundation, and homes for orphaned or homeless young girls. When I visited Hungary for the first time, I prompted my relatives for opportunities to contribute and volunteered at a homeless clinic next door to an academic institution in downtown Budapest.

There are, of course, other ways I give back in other countries or places around the US. When disaster struck in Mexico City and Puerto Rico, I fueled the local economy and engaged with the locals on how I could be most helpful. Throughout 2020, I gave my time to support the overall message behind the Black Lives Matter movement by spreading anti-racism and love for Black and Indigenous people of color while in the streets of DC. I also collaborated with people across the US in Arizona, Vermont, Illinois, New York, New Jersey, and

Georgia by inviting discussion and compiling anti-racism resources.

THE FOUR WORLD-CHANGING FORCES

It is important to relish the journey embedded within each mindset. The Giving Back mindset is the closest to the world-changing forces and represents a readiness to act more sustainably on your travels, but it would be a missed opportunity to jump all the way to this mindset without first navigating the other three. Each mindset builds on the other and also serves as a feedback loop the more you travel. For example, if I remain open-minded to others' perspectives, I will find out the truth about their experiences. If I find out the truth about myself, I will be able to grow personally and develop the resilience needed to navigate the inherent risks associated with traveling.

I can be most effective as a global activist or global citizen once I take the time to find out the truth of what makes me and others happy, keep an open mind to learning what aspects of my travels are unsustainable, and develop the resilience to apply lessons learned.

I have a lifetime of intentional travel behind me and in front of me that I can measure for impact toward the four world-changing forces. As I reflect on the ultimate outcome of the infinity symbol, I envision it to represent endless love and connection with others. I realize that our generation (the new class of 2020) has graduated from the hatred, racism, and inequities we experience in the world, which is our infinity war.

We are here to avenge our brothers and sisters so that our endgame isn't a mere half of humanity, but rather one where all of us can coexist in love and acceptance as a global society. While my journey exploring the sustainable travel mindsets has culminated in me traveling the world as a global activist against racism and prioritizing promoting cultural awareness as my world-changing force, you may decide to start with reducing your carbon footprint in the name of climate change so that you can save our planet from our destructive habits.

You may also decide the first half of this formula should be replaced by your own mindset principles. As long as they lead to the same world-changing outcomes and others can repeat and sustain them in the long run, in the vein of sustainable transit, I say full steam ahead. Be sure to take all the time you need to reflect on your travel experiences as you create and explore your own sustainable travel mindsets.

Whatever your purpose, this book will entertain your out-of-the-box ideas about traveling while guiding you through the strategies you can take to leave more positive footprints behind.

PART II

FINDING TRUTH

*Racism has historically been a banner to justify the
enterprises of expansion, conquest, colonization,
and domination and has walked hand in hand
with intolerance, injustice, and violence.*

-RIGOBERTA MENCHÚ TUM, GUATEMALAN INDIGENOUS
LEADER AND NOBEL PEACE PRIZE LAUREATE

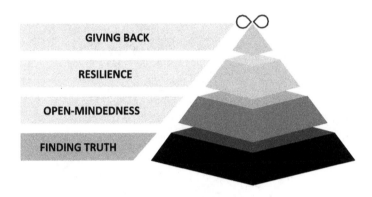

Finding Truth positions you to learn and absorb as much as you can about yourself and others in the context of your respective places in the world. This mindset embodies a state of understanding before reacting or acting on our biases toward cultures or lifestyles foreign to us. We should spend the most time and effort in this stage prior to embarking on our travels.

CHAPTER 3

AN UNEQUAL WORLD

As I crossed the Arlington Memorial Bridge with the Lincoln Memorial in front of me, I could feel the energy of people gathered from around the country. We were all gathered there in unity and peace for the #GetYourKneeOffOurNecks March on Washington to commemorate the Great March on Washington led by American civil rights activist Dr. Martin Luther King, Jr. At the 1963 march, King called for equal right and an end to racism during his iconic "I Have a Dream" speech, which prompted the end of Jim Crow segregation laws and unequal policies around voting.

Attracting one of the largest national turnouts of the year, the march represented a catharsis of all the grief and anger that had boiled up from the summer of protesting for Black lives. History was repeating itself in 2020 with the onslaught of police brutality to unarmed Black men and women and protestors, harkening back to the bloody marches of the 1960s civil rights movement.

Weeks later, our 2016-elected president, Donald J. Trump, signed an executive order expressly denying the existence of inherent racism within government systems.[11] Under that premise, he banned the use of federal grant funds for the "blame-focused diversity training" of the federal workforce or uniformed services.[12] Such programs "perpetuate racial stereotypes and division," argued Trump, by blaming individuals of one race or gender for the past actions of members of their race or gender.[13] To continue to subject White men to any training or education that might make them feel guilty or uncomfortable for their Whiteness would, according to the order, create a hostile work environment. Trump's Executive Order on Combating Race and Sex Stereotyping banned the US military from teaching "our heroic men and women in uniform the lie that the country for which they are willing to die is fundamentally racist."[14] With the stroke of a pen, Trump pulled grant money from any program that even suggested the existence of racism, unconscious bias, and gender disparities.[15] His administration had been chipping away at fifty-seven years of hard-won progress toward civil rights and now commenced to take a wrecking ball to it.

I can hear the denial from Trump supporters now, desperately defending his actions while avoiding the larger issue of racism.

---

11 White House, "Executive Order on Combating Race and Sex Stereotyping," September 22, 2020.

12 Ibid.

13 Ibid.

14 Ibid.

15 White House, "Executive Order on Combating Race and Sex Stereotyping," September 22, 2020.

During the 2020 presidential debates, Trump found himself with nowhere to run from the issue. Debate moderator Chris Wallace and Trump's Democratic challenger, former Vice President Joe Biden, pressed the president to denounce White supremacy and take an active stance against racism. Trump faltered and refused.

Trump's refusal to denounce White supremacy—live on national television—drew an indelible line between racists and anti-racists. His supporters' continued loyalty to him made it clear to me which side of the line they occupied.

In my conversations with several Trump supporters, I would say, "I can tell you firsthand that racism still exists today."

As for their own denial, supporters would argue, "The past is in the past, and slavery happened in the past. It's no longer relevant today."

Tell that to the millions of African Americans who still carry the last name of a slave owner.

WHAT'S IN A NAME?

What's in a name, you ask?

Words and names rooted in our history can commemorate a historical or familial figure, inspire a message, or even launch a movement. They can also represent an assimilation to culture for better or worse.

This is certainly the case with the immigrants that changed their last names at Ellis Island and also speaks to my personal experience. When I was seven, our family changed our last name from Suravarapu to Surio, partly so America could easily pronounce it.

Alternatively, I've seen some Black people in America change their last name in favor of cultural names to signify their commitment to breaking the forced legacy from the slave owner.

One such example brought about a legacy that would inspire generations to come and started with an Indigenous activist in Peru.

* * *

Walking through the faded pastel colored museum, images and sculptures associated with key moments in Peruvian history eagerly awaited my curiosity for the hidden mysteries of the Incas. I did a double take as I recognized a name, Tupac. I immediately wondered why the name of the late global hip-hop icon was in a museum in Cusco, Peru. Peruvian Tupac's history came long before Tupac Shakur made a name for himself under that same moniker. I wanted to better understand the origins of his name. Tupac Amaru's full name, etched into the plastic placard on the wall, hailed from Quechuan, an Indigenous language spoke in Peru and the Andes. As I continued walking, I noticed a tribute to a second Tupac Amaru. The first Tupac Amaru ruled as the last Sapa Inca ruler of the Cusco Kingdom. Tupac Amaru II, who bore no relation to the ruler, chose to assume the name as he led the largest uprising of Indigenous Spanish American people in the history of their colony and became known as a Peruvian revolutionary during the eighteenth century. Tupac Amaru II became a symbol for global insurgence following the 1960s–1970s "global fascination with third world political struggles and anti-colonialism."[16]

As I reveled in this discovery, I wanted to dig deeper into whether Tupac Shakur had some deeper connection to Peru.

I learned that Tupac Shakur's mother, Afeni Shakur changed her three-year-old son's name from Lesane Parish Crooks to the Quechuan name Tupac, to pay respect to Indigenous people engaged in the fight for freedom all over the world. Afeni, a Black Panther and revolutionary herself, thought it fitting the legacy of her son should be a global representation of nonconformity and resistance.[17] She was right. Twenty-four years after Tupac—revered by fans as 2Pac—died of gunshot wounds, his music and message continue to inspire and resonate with people of all walks of life, including 2020 Democratic vice presidential candidate Senator Kamala Harris. While the Republican party worked to discredit and mock Senator Harris for noting that 2Pac was her favorite rapper alive, even though he's been deceased for over two decades, I

---

16   Charles Walker, Berkeley Review of Latin American Studies, Fall 2014, Peru: Reflections of Tupac Amaru (Berkley, CA: University of California Berkley: Center for Latin American Studies, 2014).

17   Janice Llamoca, "The Secret Revolutionary History of Tupac Shakur's Name," TrackRecord, June 23, 2017.

have another interpretation for Harris' answer.[18] 2Pac's spirit remains alive whenever we rap, listen to, or quote his lyrics, especially in the name of resisting oppression. With that in mind, I smiled at the irony behind the words of Trump/Pence reelection campaign senior adviser, Jason Miller, as he stated, "I can confirm that we have left a ticket [to the 2020 vice presidential debate] for Tupac Shakur, who as we know is Senator Harris' favorite rapper alive."[19] Indeed, I hope 2Pac's spirit of resistance was with us that night and continues to inspire the hearts and minds of all who seek justice.

A SENSE OF DISPLACEMENT

In thinking about the impact of the past, I found myself hungry for the truth. And in thinking about sustainability in how we navigate our world today, with the understanding that racism is still rampant even outside America, I grappled with where to begin.

To what extent do we, as a globalized society, need to understand how things began?

As I thought about the tragedy that is not knowing your true last name, I found that America's history was more poignant

---

18 Reuters Staff, "Fact check: Kamala Harris did not say she listened to Snoop Dogg and Tupac while smoking marijuana in college," Reuters, August 20, 2020.

19 Dominic Patten, "Tupac Shakur Has Tix for Tonight's VP Debate Thanks to Mike Pence in Dig at Kamala Harris Calling Dead Icon Her Favorite Living Rapper," Deadline, October 7, 2020.

than ever in perpetuating global racism because of centuries of leadership failing to denounce it.

Exploration and colonization of the new world, closely accompanied by racism, quickly escalated to massacres, forced-march relocations, rapes, and death by starvation/disease.[20]

From 1514 to 1866, the transatlantic slave trade uprooted close to twenty million Africans. According to the Slave Voyages Project, most of the men, women, and children enslaved during that time had roots in West Africa and West Central Africa, while others hailed from parts of Eastern Africa.[21]

Some scholars estimate that by 1800, Africa's population was half what it would have been without the slave trades. This depletion of human resources impacted Africa's ability to flourish. Many slaves were captured through kidnappings, raids, and warfare from colonizers, which ultimately weakened each African countries' institutions in addition to their social and economic development.

One example is the Kongo Kingdom, which used to trade diverse products with the Portuguese, including copper, ivory, textiles, and slaves. Slaves traded were originally prisoners of war or criminals. However, the Portuguese demanded more slaves due to internal country politics and competition for the throne, which resulted in a dramatic and uncontrolled

---

20 Emory University, Center for Digital Scholarship, "Slave Voyages Project," accessed June 2, 2020.

21 Ibid.

increase in the capture of slaves and resulting raids throughout Kongo. The Kongo King wrote to the King of Portugal that Portuguese merchants were colluding with some of their noblemen to illegally enslave their Kongolese citizens, and in 1526 he requested the removal of all Portuguese merchants. His efforts were unsuccessful as slave-raiding continued largely unchecked well into the sixteenth century, which then ultimately culminated in a civil war that resulted in the collapse of the Kingdom. Kongo used to be located in western-central Africa in what is now the modern-day Democratic Republic of the Congo (DRC), and Angola and the Kongolese are essentially the ancestors of the Congolese, so named with a C due to the Portuguese translation.[22]

The effects of slavery in DRC are still felt today as the number of Congolese migrants and refugees leaving or being forced to leave continues to increase over a period of four decades.[23] DRC, one of Africa's richest in resources, still remains one of the least developed countries in the world.[24] Beyond that, many Congolese that have moved to other parts of Africa and beyond, have had to grow up without knowing what it means to be from DRC.

As I think about the story of my Congolese-American friend, Ndaya Cynthia, who grew up in a refugee camp outside of DRC, I realize that the bravery and resilience she portrays

---

22   Ibid.

23   Marie-Laurence Flahaux and Bruno Schoumaker, "Democratic Republic of the Congo: A Migration History Marked by Crises and Restrictions," Migration Policy Institute, April 20, 2016.

24   Ibid.

is mirrored by the millions of other Congolese who have endured the same. This story represents their global experience, and in my experience, who they are in the face of tragedy. Ndaya defined her own cultural identity as a child refugee resettling to America and learned that the traumatic experiences of children living in refugee camps could become their psychological identity. From her story, I learned how the history of the destruction of the Kingdom of Kongo, rooted in the greed for slavery, resulted in political and territorial unrest, which affected the Congolese sense of identity and place.

It was maddening to learn about how most children are only looking to heal and learn about themselves outside of their experiences in the camp. What Ndaya found through her own journey of understanding her identity is that most child refugees have to construct an identity from embracing their experiences, both in the refugee camp and in their new home country. Unfortunately, the less ambiguous a country's culture, the less room for uniqueness and more restrictive their new home country might be in requiring that immigrants assimilate, even if what that means is hard to define.

Ndaya believes the Western world could better demonstrate and embrace the true nature of their reality in being a diverse nation of people from different backgrounds and countries. If America fully embraces this ideal, she believes it would make it easier for refugee children, or even immigrant and first-generation Americans, to integrate easily with society.

On a massive scale, this sense of displacement is exactly what Black Americans face every day, not knowing their home country in Africa or even being able to reconcile what happened to their ancestors, to the extent they know the history of those ancestors. Once I knew these truths, I was inspired to make right these wrongs and check to see what privileges were earned versus stolen.

TRAVELING AS A PERSON OF COLOR IN AMERICA

If we think to the first African slaves, they were forced to step foot on our lands because the alternative was facing an ocean that stood in the way of returning to their homeland. From there, the enslaved continued to hope and support movements from the Underground Railroad, to abolishing slavery, to combatting Jim Crow and segregation, to the civil rights movement, and more recently the protests and marches for the Black Lives Matter movement. As we uncover this truth, we begin to understand this has been a near constant fight for the better part of America's young history. And as Americans, the majority of us are still upholding systems that don't work for all, especially not those who are Black and Brown in this country.

While still navigating a Jim Crow south, one Black postman, Victor Green, had found a way to remain open-minded and challenge his deep-rooted fears about America by finding Black-owned businesses that offered places to stay or eat. He documented these locations in a manifesto called The Green Book.[25] The Green Book was the most comprehensive guide for African Americans who were traveling throughout the

25   Victor Green, The Negro Motorist Green-Book: 1940 Facsimile Edition
     (Independently published, 1936).

US as it included places to eat, to fellowship, to stay, and to seek out safety should they run into trouble while driving or traveling across the country.[26] Unfortunately, Candacy Taylor's quest for Green Book sites some fifty years later during her road trip throughout America resulted in the discovery that less than 5 percent of businesses remained intact or were operational.[27] She wrote her experiences on the road, including what she encountered, in her book, Overground Railroad.[28]

"It's . . . a pilgrimage toward understanding a country so blinded by symbolism that it can't or won't tackle the . . . relentless forces that created the environment for the Green Book to thrive in the first place [and] shows . . . why after all this time, we still have so far to go," states Taylor about her book.[29]

We look at these resources not as past history, but as an opportunity to bring these Green Book sites and the rich history of Black travel in America back to our future.

---

26   Ibid.

27   Candacy Taylor, Overground Railroad: The Green Book and the Roots of Black Travel in America (New York: Abrams Press, 2020).

28   Ibid.

29   Ibid.

EXPERIENCING RACISM IN AMERICA

The first time I experienced racism was in Florida, which includes a fraught history of slavery as part of the Confederate South.[30]

There are those who see no harm in the confederate flags waving from the driveways of those in my hometown. In my experience, it's a representation of someone who celebrates the history of slavery that the Confederacy was created to uphold.

This celebration of the Confederacy didn't stop with memorabilia either. On the contrary, it encouraged acts of racism.

Racism plagued my childhood and teenage years. On one particular occasion, I remember hearing a neighbor's mother refer to me as a jezebel despite not knowing me that well. Jezebels are viewed as lascivious, hyper-sexual, and a bad influence.[31] On other occasions, people misunderstood me because I am different. Most people would generalize that I was either Black, Hispanic, both, or worse, Christopher Columbus' ill-defined labeling of the indigenous tribes of this nation as Indians. For those unfamiliar, Columbus thought he had arrived in India when he first came to the country we call America, and as such, he mislabeled the indigenous people as Indians. Over time, my experience morphed from

---

30 Emory University, Center for Digital Scholarship, "Slave Voyages Project."

31 K. Sue Jewell, From mammy to Miss America and beyond: Cultural images and the shaping of US social policy, 1st Edition (London, United Kingdom: Routledge & CRC Press, 1992).

racism and misunderstanding to fetishizing my culture because it was considered "exotic."

While on my travels, I experience or witness this same fascination with otherness followed by murmurs of the word "exotic" by travelers who are from a fairly homogenous community or country, and usually, not people of color.

Even as a little girl, once I'd learned the true story of Christopher Columbus, I was fueled with energy to question and challenge others' motivations for lifting up a certain group of people. I also took this energy with me to the frontlines of the Washington, DC protests in early summer 2020. I considered Washington, DC to be one of the most progressive cities in the world, so it angered me that I was met with ignorance and racism there. Until that summer, the racism I had encountered in DC was of the nuanced, baked-into-bureaucracy variety. Now it was all out in the open, and the world was watching. Amid the chaos of the protests and the danger of a face-off with law enforcement officers, fellow peaceful protestors and I linked up peacefully. We came together, again and again, that summer to stand in unity alongside the Black community in support of Black lives.

TRAVELING AS A PERSON OF COLOR ABROAD

Christina, a born-and-bred proud young Black woman from Maryland, USA, has always been intrigued by South America and Hispanic culture. When she first visited South America, she was overwhelmed with gratitude by the welcoming nature of the Colombian and Brazilian locals she engaged. They treated her like an Afro-Latina daughter and identified her as one of their own, even though it wasn't her own culture. The more she embraced their way of life, the more she realized that aspects of it strongly resonated. She experienced cultural practices rooted in African culture. For example, she received the Band Timbalada's tribal motif body painting, a practice which traces back to initiation marks from the Candomble religion and is now widely regarded as a cultural symbol in Bahia, Brazil. She also took part in another tradition where she tied colorful bands around her wrists at the historical cathedral in Pelourinho Salvador, where mostly Afro-Brazilian descendants live.

Christina lives and works as a diplomat in Brazil. Recognizing elements of her own privilege as a Black American abroad, she is doing her part to not play tourist but instead dig deeper to understand and interact with other Afro-descendants of Candeal and Pelourinho Salvador, Bahia, Brazil. They have quickly become her community, her people.

Meanwhile, hundreds of miles away, a first-generation Ethiopian-American, Meron, geared up to explore her roots in Africa when she accepted a work fellowship in Addis Ababa, Ethiopia. While Los Angeles is where she has lived most of her life, she felt right at home as she navigated Addis Ababa public transit to and from work like a local. She had opportunities to connect with family that lived in the city and spent a significant time understanding her role in the African diaspora as a first-generation American. This experience also inspired her to seek African experiences on her trip to Paris.

"There's this perception of what Paris is supposed to look and feel like as the city of love," and yet "I was also aware that they ravaged Africa. I knew, for better or worse, of large local Francophone-African communities in Paris, and I was curious to learn more and engage with them."

She and a friend looked up African restaurants and met with a restaurant owner from Djibouti who shared his recommendations on African neighborhoods and markets.

"When we went there, it felt like a different place that you don't always get to hear about or see. I felt proud to be an African here," just as the people were proud.

There were aspects of French culture that these communities chose to embrace and make their own, as Francophone-Africans. Given these two very African experiences, it is no surprise that I saw her on the frontlines of the Black Lives Matter protests in LA with thousands of others. After all, Meron's name holds cultural significance in Ethiopia as holy anointed one and in Hebrew translates to soldier. As an African-American, her light and fight shine through as she continues to support her African and Black brothers and sisters in solidarity.

CHECK YOUR PRIVILEGES

While there are hundreds more stories I could tell, from navigating the world as a person of color to navigating the tragedies at home in America, it's longer than can fit in this book alone. Ultimately, it is up to you as the reader to find out the truth as you learn about different people around the world and their experience with racism in other countries. It is also your responsibility to dig as deep into the history as might be necessary to uncover how it still plays a role in the modern world.

Once you know the truth, you can practice checking yourself on the privileges you have and which others don't because of racism and its reverberating impacts, which have continued to be passed down, upheld, and protected. In failing to check privilege, invisible walls erect because some find it too hard to deal with the shame or lack the empathy to recognize why they should care.

Whether you are coming from a place of ignorance or intentionally engaging in racist actions, the call to action is the same.

- Find and read the stories of people who have experienced an unequal world.
- Ask yourself what stereotypes and prejudices you have toward others.
- Check your privileges to see if you are upholding an unequal world.

I think again of Tupac and how he stood up against conformity, speaking the truth in his internationally celebrated lyrics. He represents the opposite of maintaining the status quo, and we should be inspired to do the same in an unequal world.

CHAPTER 4

GLOBALIZATION: AN ORIGIN STORY OF THIRD CULTURE KIDS OF THE WORLD

———

"I've never felt more un-American in my life."

"But then, when have we ever truly felt American?"

"I couldn't agree more," I said.

Earlier that day, my friends and I had spent eight hours engaging in one of America's most defining activities: exercising our constitutional right to free speech. Now gathered around a living room table, we began to unpack our experiences as third culture kids (TCK), first-generation Americans, and participants in the 2020 March on Washington.

To march among thousands of people and speak in one voice as a sea of Black, Brown, and White is unifying. At the same time, as I think about my experiences in an unequal world, I am caught between the privileges associated with my family's choice to come to this country and the fact that my skin color invites racism from those who continue to remain ignorant about the multiplicity that is my ethnicity.

I wondered, Why don't we feel at home here?

I attribute this to globalism, the ever-increasing interdependence between economies and connections among world cultures, but which not everyone is open to.

Some scholars trace globalization back to the development of the Silk Road, 4,000 miles of trade routes connecting China to other parts of Asia, the Middle East, and Europe.[32] "Threads of a web formed over millennia, with the number and reach . . . increasing over time. People, money, material goods, ideas, disease, and devastation have traveled these silken strands . . . in greater numbers and with greater speed."[33]

There were some routes, like the Royal Road, which opened trade between Persia, India, and parts of Egypt and Mesopotamia in operation 300 years before the Silk Road but

---

32 "Silk Road," History Channel, A&E Television Networks, LLC., last updated September 26, 2019.

33 "Globalization," National Geographic, Encyclopedia, Resource Library, accessed September 20, 2020.

incorporated into its network of trade routes.[34] These routes have had a lasting impact on increasing the connectedness of countries as it relates to culture, commerce, and history.

While we've explored the negative impacts of exploration and connectedness in how an unequal world was created, there are positive results, one of which is the emergence of TCKs.

Speaking from the perspective of a TCK, I am the product of ancestors who took the first step to cross an ocean to pursue life elsewhere while maintaining that connection to their heritage. With the opportunities to study and work abroad, my parents, who hail from different backgrounds, met in the city of brotherly love, Philadelphia, and I was born.

In finding my own unique voice and identity, I've met other TCKs and realized the important role we play in paving the way toward positive globalization and the bridging of cultures.

The increasing trend toward globalization due to people leaving their home country to live or explore another has given rise to our existence.

* * *

Even as we take pride in being American, I think it's important for us to take time to learn the challenges that continue to face immigrants to this country, especially those from certain countries. In the name of nationalism, the 2017

---

34   "Silk Road," History Channel.

presidential executive order banned immigrants, short and long-term visa holders, and for a limited time, green card holders who came from a specific country.[35]

Can you imagine temporarily leaving America as a green card holder and not being able to get back in?

Perhaps you left your home country to come to America as my father did.

My father had eyes on America since childhood. Western movies gained immense popularity in India around the time my father was born, and as a pastime, his family would go to the local theatre in the village. Seeing the promise of freedom and an open road full of adventure, America stuck with my father as he grew into a young adult. He searched for opportunities to study abroad in America, certain that this would get him the golden ticket to stay and pursue citizenship.

Had US President Ronald Reagan signed an executive order banning immigrants from India at the time, my father may not have set up roots in this country. Half a world away, a young Indian man would board a plane, land in the US, and be denied entry. When I ask my father about his journey, he mentions how he easily could have ended up in Canada had he not met my mother. She provided an opportunity, through their union, for a path to citizenship. My father may not have been my father, or it's possible I would be Canadian instead! My Indian-Canadian cousin, Sonika, would have no qualms

---

35   White House, "Executive Order Protecting the Nation from Foreign Terrorist Entry into the United States," January 27, 2017.

with that! However, it's just as plausible that my father would have gone back to India to work, as he was receiving immense pressure from his own father and family to return.

For those privileged by their citizenship, socioeconomic background, or political clout, achieving your dreams in America is possible. However, for others, even the first step of coming to America can be riddled with hardships and family separations, with no guarantee of being treated equally.

Moreover, Black and Indigenous people missed out on opportunities to achieve the American dream since the inception of America's history. Throughout our history, European and then White Americans, stole Indigenous tribes' land and African people to perpetuate a racist system that would serve them. With the current state of police brutality and ongoing racial unrest in our country, I understand why some of my closest Black friends wish to leave or consider dual citizenship in Africa as a fail-safe to a less tolerant America.

With a majority of family connections outside of America, we don't get to experience the large family reunions and stories around the dinner table unless we take a flight abroad. Our family in Dubai, India, and Hungary face obstacles in visiting us due to financial barriers and complications applying for and receiving a visa to enter the country. When I get on a plane to visit them, I don't have to think about these barriers due to the privilege inherent in my American passport.

CITIZENSHIP CHALLENGES

The cold temperatures of Dubai's desert winter creep in the night like a shadow as one woman closes the window before resuming her place at the kitchen table with the other women. The men's voices and laughter crescendo from the dining room, where they belly up to the table to share ice cream and happy memories from times in Visakhapatnam, a small beach town in Andhra Pradesh, India. Their separation is emblematic of the cultural divide, but as an American, I sit with the men to discuss their latest topic of travel to America.

One woman brings around Falooda, one of my favorite Indian desserts, a colorful mix of ice cream, yogurt, jellied sweets, and fruit. I encourage the woman to join us in the discussion, but she politely declines, and I wonder why they aren't more engaged in the conversation.

The resignation in the voice of one young man snaps me back to the conversation as he details his struggles with citizenship.

"I don't know what I'll do because my visa expires next year."

He expands on the difficulty of applying for citizenship as he toys with the idea of returning to India if unsuccessful.

The process is lengthy. It includes a lengthy application, a sponsor letter of invitation to justify why they need to visit America, and the cost of applying for every member of the household.

Because Indians do not have permanent citizenship in Dubai, getting a visa to visit America presents challenges due to the ambiguity of their citizenry.

Frustrated when I hear about these barriers to entry, I am reminded of the citizenship struggles of Indian people in Madagascar.

I think to myself, Why do my people experience this so frequently?

Indian settlers who crossed the Indian Ocean as traders to Madagascar continue to face immense challenges in securing citizenship. One hundred and fifty years ago, Indian settlers arrived in Madagascar and built a life for themselves, comprising 20,000 of the population.[36] The entire country has twenty-six million people. The majority of the population's ethnicity is Malagasy, which means they are the descendants of Malayo-Indonesians and Africans.[37] Karan, who is also Indian, shared how, despite their strong ties to Madagascar, Indians are not considered citizens. While the Indians of Madagascar, also known as Karanas, are more "cosmopolitan, it also means they belong nowhere and everywhere." [38]

Furthermore, Malagasy people hold onto stereotypes about Indians that keep the two mostly separated, especially when it comes to interracial relationships.

---

36 Karan Mahajan, "Stateless," Airbnb Magazine, December/January 2020 Issue, p. 127–137.

37 Ibid.

38 Ibid.

Madagascar has one of the most restrictive citizenship regimens in the world. Naturalization is nonexistent because the requirement is that you must be of Malagasy descent. This leaves Indians who live in Madagascar without a pathway to citizenship. People of Indian descent who live in Madagascar are also not considered Indian citizens.

One example of this is the story of Rames Abhukara, now retired diplomat over seventy, whose life has, in part, revolved around the question of citizenship.

"When I was seventeen. . . a few friends and I decided to hitchhike and go to Africa." [39]

This dream evaporated when Rames went to the passport office, and the government official didn't view him as Malagasy. The official did not grant him travel documents to continue on his journey. At this point, Rames realized he was paperless, and he decided to petition the British, Indian, and French embassies for citizenship documents. [40]

At the Indian embassy, officials said he was ineligible for citizenship. They directed him to the British embassy, as his father had arrived in Madagascar when India was still a British colony. They considered Rames a British subject.

When approaching the British embassy, officials redirected him back to the Indian embassy, citing India's independence as proof enough of his Indian citizenship.

---

39 Ibid.

40 Ibid.

India continued to route him elsewhere.

At one point, France offered Karanas citizenship once French rule of Madagascar ended in the 1960s, but one had to know the ins and outs of applying.[41] At the time, Rames' father did not know how to navigate the citizenship process as a poor farmer, so they remained stateless.

For Rames and many Karanas, citizenship is a winding, narrow road up a mountain whose peak never comes into the frame.

It is worth noting that banning whole countries not only impacts their desire or ability to fuel our economy, but also turns off those of us who have traveled the world and know better. Many people feel this disillusionment as they decide to leave America or continue to ponder whether to visit. It dissuades my relatives in Dubai from visiting us in America and fuels my friend's decision to remain an expatriate in China.

THE EXPAT

"I found love in this pandemic," said my Nigerian-American friend, Marshall, from his flat in Beijing, China. "I like that she's traditional Chinese [but] still very open-minded."

I am happy for him.

It has been over two years since Marshall made the move from San Francisco, California to Beijing, China to teach

---

41   Ibid.

English. He left for this new chapter of his life, disgruntled by America, alone and unsure of what he would find. Now he has found a special someone with whom to share that life. As the product of an interracial relationship myself, my mother Hungarian and my father South Indian, I smile when I hear about or see two people from different backgrounds dating. Similarly,

Marshall is the product of an interracial relationship; his mother is Caucasian, and his father is Nigerian.

I first met Marshall on a three-month study abroad and service-learning trip to Hyderabad, India. We remain good friends and stay in touch since our days of trekking through India.

Periodically, I keep up with Marshall's life and adventures abroad from Southeast Asia to Colombia. Marshall had wanted to leave America for awhile. Marshall searched for meaningful purpose amid navigating the realities of being Black in America. When Marshall lived in the Bay area, he also witnessed what he describes as a stark contrast between rich Silicon Valley acolytes and the homeless population, who could no longer afford to live in San Francisco due to increasing housing prices.

Marshall toyed with the idea of leaving America to live and work abroad. He researched potential career opportunities for an expat and decided to teach English. He then began the complicated journey of finding the right company, applying for a visa, and getting all the necessary vaccinations. Marshall says it was worth the long-suffering journey.

He has tried new things he wouldn't have tried before, like bungee jumping off a bridge or visiting historical places he normally wouldn't have found enticing due to overcrowding and tourism.

Marshall's story has come full circle. As a young child, Marshall would visit Nigeria with his father to attend functions and events with the community. These cultural experiences ended when Marshall's father died. From there, much of his life was spent in the suburbs of Northern California around a large majority of White Americans.

Marshall continued to long for experiences in other countries. His passion for cultures fueled his desire to travel abroad and learn as much as he could. Marshall has rooted his sense of community and culture not solely in his American upbringing but also in his varied experiences in Nigeria, India, Singapore, Colombia, and now China. After a conversation with Marshall about TCKs, I asked if he identifies as one.

"Yeah, I guess I am. Aren't you?"

You're probably wondering why I call out America and share the story of someone who left my home country. I call out these issues because I care about making America a better country and encourage people to stay to be a part of the solution. At the same time, I completely understand those who wish to leave in search of a better life, which for them, may mean happiness and purpose outside these borders.

Can we really fault people for leaving?

What we—the kids and grandkids of immigrants—find is that the grass is not greener. Grass can be green wherever you water, care for, and nourish it. Beyond that, if America drives people away, this speaks volumes about the current state of affairs of this country. America is not making people feel at home.

Marshall's experiences as an expatriate represents his choice to semi-permanently or permanently live in a different country or countries from his birthplace in America. Whenever immigrants live in another country, they tend to adopt the country's cultural norms and customs and may even go so far as to get dual citizenship or permanent citizenship. This is certainly the case for many of the immigrants who left their home to come and live in America. In that instance, I think about how immigrants had to decide what elements of their culture to keep versus which ones to modify in raising their kids in this country. It's this mixing of cultures and norms that we as their kids have to wade through when figuring out our own identities as Americans.

THE IMMIGRANT AND FIRST-GENERATION AMERICANS
The idea of creating one's cultural identity tends to also reveal itself in people who have dual citizenship or move as an immigrant from one country to another. Knowing my own parents had childhood experiences outside of America, I sought out what the immigrant experience was like and how people might consider their relationship between the two places.

Victor, my friend from Nigeria who has lived in America for over two decades, shared stories about taking trips to Nigeria at least once or twice a year. He embarked on these trips to check in with family and maintain a direct connection with his African heritage, but even so, he found challenges in feeling at home.

"I feel like a visitor [because] I am not ingrained in the communities' day to day . . . [I'm] more of an outsider," he said.

Similarly, my Nigerian-American friend, Janet, opened up about growing up with immigrant parents in America.

"Where do I stand out as American? [Where] do I adopt Nigerian characteristics?" she asked, as we spoke about what it means to be a first-generation American.

We spoke at length about the duality of being both African and Black in America. Janet noted how the buzz generated by the larger global Black community around one of my all-time favorite Marvel movies, *Black Panther*, dismantled problematic and stereotypical narratives about Africa.[42]

I had to agree with her. The film demonstrated the world's tendency to view countries in Africa in the opening scenes where Wakanda is portrayed as an impoverished third world country.

---

42 *Black Panther*, directed by Ryan Coogler, written by Ryan Coogler and Joe Robert Cole, (Burbank, CA: Marvel Studios, 2018), film.

The audience finds out that it's a thriving, futuristic metropolis representing Black Power.[43] Black Panther has helped change the image and perception of Africa for many Americans. Janet emphasizes how we need more opportunities to share and celebrate African culture in America.

"Some Africans critique [the movie]," she said, "and say it's not a real representation of Africa, it's not [based on] a real country. But I think it's positive. It offers representation for people who look like me. It spurred more Black Americans to seek out and explore [their] roots in Africa."

Janet has had opportunities to visit her native country of Nigeria in Africa.

Recognizing her privilege as a Black woman to know and travel to her native country, she continues to seek opportunities to teach Americans about Nigerian culture. She doesn't want her connection to her culture to be lost even as she plans to continue to live in America. Recently, she's been learning Igbo, her tribal tongue.

When in Nigeria, Janet also learned there are aspects of American culture, such as our openness to tipping for good service, that are very different from what she observed in Nigeria. For example, while her cousins encouraged her that it wasn't necessary to tip the house chef for his service, she felt compelled to tip him. Tipping domestic workers is not a common practice in Nigeria.

---

43   Ibid.

Janet also shared that while her parents stressed the importance of her being Nigerian-American, she found that in school, it wasn't cool or as popular to identify with one's ethnic roots. So, she distanced herself from it in middle and high school. In college, she explored her roots by taking several trips to Nigeria and enrolling in African American studies courses to learn about the history of the African diaspora in America.

Each trip to Nigeria provides Janet with a better sense of awareness, pride, and respect for her culture, which continues to strengthen through her adulthood.

"Every time I've gone, it's strengthened my connection. I'm just incredibly grateful for that and that my parents championed me being Nigerian and took me to cultural family parties growing up. I've grown to love and really appreciate my Nigerian heritage. As part of the Nigerian diasporan, I feel obligated to move my culture forward by elevating our culture, customs, and values."

I thought about how that applied to my experience growing up. My parents emphasized that I needed to speak English well to succeed. When I went to school, and no one spoke Hungarian, my first language, it made me want to stop speaking the language. As a result, my ability to speak the language faded over time because I spoke so little of it at home. It wasn't until I visited Hungary for the first time in college that I was intentional about only communicating in Hungarian, and since then, I've explored opportunities to speak the language with family abroad to maintain that fluency.

My experiences with the unkindness of racism due to my skin color and features encouraged me to seek out others, like me, who have had similar experiences. Since then, I've learned that my inability to fit in is a common characteristic of TCKs because we balance multiple identities and may represent a small minority in the world, if not the first of our kind.

I first learned about TCKs in Hawaii while on a work trip where I learned the origin story of our forty-fourth President, Barack Obama. His Kenyan father met his White American mother while studying on the island of Oahu in Hawaii. Hawaii's birth records process is distinct from the other forty-nine states. It allows citizens to identify by their ethnic heritage instead of checking a box with a prescriptive race. President Obama's birth certificate lists Kenyan and Caucasian. Because of this difference, President Obama's citizenship, including whether he was born in America, was questioned by his dissidents.

THIRD CULTURE KIDS

TCKs are children who spend most of their childhood or developmental years in a place that is not their parents' homeland or culture. The TCK will "build relationships to all cultures, while not having full ownership in any, [though] elements from each culture are assimilated into the TCKs life experiences."[44] Their sense of belonging tends to be in

---

44 "TCK World proudly presents: Dr. Ruth Hill Useem—the sociologist/ anthropologist who first coined the term "Third Culture Kid" (TCK),"

building relationships with others of the same background, or essentially other TCKs.[45]

The term TCK, first coined in the 1950s by US sociologist Dr. Ruth Hill Useem, originated while she lived in India conducting research on those who had received higher education in a Western country. The Useems returned to India in 1958 to study overseas Americans in India and took their children with them to live abroad, which initiated the concept of third culture kids.[46] Dr. Useem believed we would see a rise in TCKs as globalization continued.

In thinking about globalization, I was curious to see if we had any data or research to back up the claim that we are becoming more interconnected. What I found was the DHL Global and NYU Stern School of Business created a Global Connectedness Index (GCI) and released yearly updates highlighting developments in "international flows of capital, trade, information, and people."[47] While the GCI dipped in 2018, in 2019, the GCI stayed close to its all-time record high in 2017. This shows a more connected world than at any other point in history with no signs of reversing the trend.

With globalization comes a mixture of ethnicities and, of course, interracial relationships, all of which can lead to a rise

---

TCK World: The Official Home of Third Culture Kids, accessed August 20, 2020.

45   Ibid.

46   Ibid.

47   "DHL Global Connectedness Index," DHL Global, accessed September 12, 2020.

in TCKs. What is the origin story of TCKs who essentially belong nowhere and everywhere at once? A few include:

- They have parents who are expat workers, foreign service officers, or military personnel.
- They have parents from different countries.
- They are attending an international school abroad or an international school in their own country.
- They have permanently moved to or have lived in different countries.
- They grew up as a refugee—within their homeland or in refugee camps—before moving to a new country.[48]

TCKs are known for developing an identity rooted in people and their cultural experiences versus places, and as such, they may consider themselves citizens of the world, depending on how widespread their network and how deep their connections with the people in these countries.[49] I was fascinated by the ability of TCKs to adopt multiple cultures as a normal fact of life and decided to explore further to see if I knew anyone who exhibited these characteristics and how they had approached various cultures.

As a TCK myself, to stand up and share my unique perspective with the world. I also think each of us has something to share with the other, hailing from various walks of life and different ethnic backgrounds. I can relate to the journey most TCKs are on while navigating their ancestral and new homes and what that means for their constructed social identities.

---

48   Kate Mayberry, "Third Culture Kids: Citizens of everywhere and nowhere."
49   Ibid.

THE PROTAGONISTS: TREVOR NOAH & LUPITA NYONGO

Trevor Noah, talk show host of "The Daily Show with Trevor Noah," is the protagonist of his own show as he curates each story, paying close attention to the message he's sharing with others. I also found that Trevor shares the stories of other TCKs I feature in this book, such as Lupita Nyong'o, who is set to play Trevor's mother in the movie adaptation of his book, Born a Crime, and also Hasan Minhaj, who worked as a correspondent on his show.[50] In his book, Trevor boldly detailed his story growing up in apartheid South Africa where a system of laws mandated the separation of races, therefore, making it illegal for his African mother and Swiss father to be in an interracial relationship, let alone have a child. He details how his father would often have to walk across the street from his mother and pretend he didn't know them. Furthermore, any threat of authority figures nearby meant that Trevor had to let go of his mother's hand and fall back as if he was an orphan so as to protect his mother from any undue punishment or questioning. Noah also notes that in much of his early life, he was hidden away indoors, where he spent time reading and inventing worlds.[51] Noah recently made a companion of the book just for young readers, to communicate his message more broadly as a TCK and mixed child under such circumstances.

"A lot of the book is about me as a young kid, growing up in South Africa and going to school. It made perfect sense to

---

50 Munachim Amah, "Lupita Nyong'o to star in movie adaptation of Trevor Noah's book 'Born A Crime," CNN News, February 22, 2018, CNN World.

51 Roman Peterson, "Hope and Humor," TimeforKids, April 9, 2019.

make a book for young readers who may be leading a similar life, just in a different country."[52]

* * *

It was early March 2014, and Lupita Nyong'o has just won an Oscar for Best Supporting Actress for 12 Years a Slave. As the audience started their round of awe-inspired clapping, two other places across the globe likewise erupted into a frenzy of calls and furious typing as people stated in their mother tongue, "She's the first." Several hours later and Mexico and Kenya both released statements that Lupita was the first Mexican and the first Kenyan actress to receive an Oscar.[53] Much to their dismay, they saw the other country's claim to her fame, and the foreign reporters started feuding. In that instance, Lupita made a conscious choice to self-identify both Kenyan and Mexican at once by stating that first and foremost, "this award belongs to me . . . [but] I've seen the quarrels over my nationality [and] I'm Kenyan and Mexican at the same time . . . I am Mexican Kenyan."[54] For each country, it was a big deal not only because she was the first national of each country to win such an award, but it also put places like Kenya, and more specifically Kisumu, where her parents are from, on the map. This win went beyond Lupita and extended to the millions of Kenyans who congratulated her as it represented western media's interest in Africa beyond the poverty, violence, and disease so prominent in the media.

---

52   Ibid.

53   Arit John, "Lupita Nyong'o Ended Kenya and Mexico's Mini-Feud Over Her Nationality," The Atlantic, March 3, 2014.

54   Ibid.

At that moment, Lupita shared her true connection with Mexico and Kenya by embracing both of their nationalities as her own, and as a result, helped raise cultural awareness while also promoting a positive image for each country. By directly embracing both nationalities and winning such an achievement, she became each country's protagonist or hero. This act also inspired hope among the millions of Kenyan and Mexican youths looking up to Lupita as a role model and ambassador of their country to the western world.

THE TRAILBLAZERS: LILLY SINGH & HASAN MINHAJ

I did a double take as I saw the cover of a book with a Brown woman on it sporting a bold red blazer and lip to match. The book, How to Be a Bawse: A Guide to Conquering Life, reflects the trailblazer that Lilly Singh is and represents how Brown women can pursue careers outside of the safety net of what our immigrant parents may expect for us.[55] Lilly certainly inspired me to continue pursuing my own dreams of writing a book and spreading my message.

Lilly didn't stop with the book.

She leveraged all of her creative talents, or what she referred to as her superpowers, to build her brand as a "multi-faceted comedian and entertainer . . . [whose] comedic and

---

55   Lilly Singh, How to Be a Bawse: A Guide to Conquering Life, (New York: Ballantine Books, 2017).

inspirational YouTube videos [amassed] over eleven million subscribers."[56]

Following her professional pursuits, she also came out as bisexual, and then NBC announced she would take over late-night host Carson Daly's time slot, which made her the only female late-night host on a major network.[57]

"An Indian-Canadian woman with her own late-night show? Now that is a dream come true," she states about her latest accomplishment.[58]

Lilly continues to be "a role model for women and girls around the globe," as a UNICEF Goodwill Ambassador through her #GirlLove "initiative to break the cycle of girl-on-girl hate and encourage positivity."[59]

* * *

Hasan Minhaj is also a trailblazer in his approach and critique of the American dream. He taught himself the art of comedy by watching others and emulating some of their most common characteristics he resonated with to create his own brand of humor. He "has a reputation for breaking

56   "Lilly Singh," UNICEF People, United Nations Children's Fund, accessed September 12, 2020.

57   Kimberly Yam, "Lilly Singh Puts 'Superwoman' Name To Rest In Emotional Instagram Post," HuffPost Entertainment, Verizon Media, last updated August 15, 2019.

58   Ibid.

59   "Lilly Singh," UNICEF People, United Nations Children's Fund.

new ground," which comes as no surprise as he's navigated three identities as a TCK who is Indian-American-Muslim.[60]

As Hasan checks in on his sense of self and identity, he wonders, "'Am I more Indian or am I more American? What part of my identity am I?'"[61]

Earlier, we spoke about the executive order ban on certain countries from entering the US. For the Minhaj family, this was a part of their reality as his parents are Muslim immigrants from Aligarh, India. After the election, Hasan was afraid his mother, who was visiting family in India, might not be able to return to the US even though she was an American citizen, because of the ban on Muslims. Hasan also notes he's battling these generational differences between his father as an immigrant and himself as a US-born citizen. He mentions that his father is from a generation, like many immigrants, where if you come to this country, you pay the American dream tax, meaning you'll endure some racism, and if it doesn't cost you your life, then you got lucky and should pay up.

For Hasan and other TCKs born in America, we have the "audacity of equality."[62]

60 David Bianculli, "Comic Hasan Minhaj On Roasting Trump And Growing Up A 'Third Culture Kid," interview by David Bianculli, Fresh Air, NPR, December 29, 2017, podcast, MP3 audio.

61 Ibid.

62 Ibid.

Hasan notes that one of the biggest disparities between immigrant parents and TCKs is that while our parents are pragmatists, we tend to be optimists and think of ourselves as equal from a young age, which means we don't want to be treated any kind of way. For Hasan, he watched his father turn a blind eye to hate crimes and had to decide for himself if he would follow in his father's footsteps and count his blessings or take that moment to speak up and say something because it is wrong.

I think I can agree with Hasan about speaking up when he says, "Being an angry optimist is the solution."[63]

THE INSTIGATOR: MATANGI (MIA)

There are times where being angry is all we may know, and it fuels us to challenge the system. This is certainly the case for worldwide pop and hip-hop artist Matangi, stage name MIA, whose sense of displacement from living in multiple countries has sensitized her to the immigrant story.

"I need to keep the immigrant story in all my work always because that is what I'm trying to make sense of," she stated, "people have always mixed, and mingled, and moved, and interesting things happen because of it."[64]

---

63   Ibid.

64   Lulu Garcia-Navarro and Sarah Handel, "It Never Existed Before': M.I.A. On Changing Pop And Documenting Her Story," interview by Lulu Garcia-Navarro, Weekend Edition Sunday, NPR, September 30, 2018, podcast, MP3 audio.

MIA is a Tamil refugee born in the United Kingdom (UK) but grew up in Sri Lanka. Her father was a Tamil Sri-Lankan engineer who tried to create an independent state for the Tamils in Sri-Lanka. His cause met with significant resistance, and as a result, he sent his family to India for several years. MIA moved around quite a bit after her first shuffle from the UK and spent several years living between Sri Lanka, UK, and America.[65]

MIA also has a dual-national son with citizenship in America and the UK. Sadly, she's unable to travel with him to America or visit him while he is there because her visa status is still pending review by the US Customs and Border Protection. MIA speculates it's because of her confrontational nature and feuding with certain managers or big names in the music industry, but hers is among the hundreds of people who are turned away from entering each day. In this example of a TCK story, MIA is someone who's never quite fully found her home. While this sense of not belonging to one place makes for great hits, like her song "Borders," MIA is adamant about tearing down the walls we put up between countries, both proverbial and literal.[66] Those who follow her story will witness someone who is still trying to find the truth of what her culture, that of an immigrant, really is. Nevertheless, she takes no pity as she boldly instigates change and controversy in her messaging.

MIA embraces her sense of no place for what it is as she keeps an ear out for the truth, both finding it and telling it,

65   Ibid.
66   Ibid.

through her music. She infuses other cultures and lifestyles into her own, most notably in the creativity of her music, which mixes elements of pop, dubstep, traditional Tamil or Indian music, hip-hop, and rap.

* * *

In my conversations with many about the concept of TCKs, furrowed eyebrows and assumptions about third world countries would emerge. Previously used as jargon, I've decided to use TCKs of the world as a symbol of where we are headed as a global society and what it might mean to start mixing cultures and customs. TCKs face a number of complexities in their identity and sense of place, some of which have no easy resolution. Perhaps this is due to the fact that TCKs are quite a new phenomenon in general, with the increasing globalization and mixing of the world. People who embrace both ethnicities are also potentially subject to feuding, criticism, or confusion as to how to wear both on their sleeve without being misunderstood. The problem with a monolithic world view or culture and the issue of Westernization, has in my experience, manifested in how we handle what we do not understand. There are people who will disagree about our mixing and trend toward globalization at the cost of its borders and who support the opposite of what TCKs represent.

I'm not here to tell you what political stance on immigration is wrong, but to encourage acceptance and empathy from the human stories shared, representing our increasingly third culture world.

For what it's worth, we are on the same side as a human species. We are all one human, whether we wish to plainly see that or not. I wonder if we can take a page out of NASA's book for a moment, the ambassadors of our planet and image to the rest of the universe. NASA sent a greeting to the universe on the Voyager spacecraft, crossing the chasms of our differences to include the things we as humans fundamentally have in common: children laughing, music, pictures, birds chirping, and greetings from fifty-five languages.[67]

While we start Part II in frustration with the state of affairs in America, my next chapter will take you through a journey of self-discovery across the US. As much as exploring the world has provided immense perspective, it was in my own backyard where I cultivated my American identity, as one of three that makeup who I am as a TCK.

67 "Greetings to the Universe in 55 Different Languages," NASA, accessed May 5, 2020.

CHAPTER 5

PURSUIT OF HAPPYNESS—A JOURNEY THROUGH AMERICA

AN EXPEDITION TO FIND HAPPYNESS

The fresh air from the open school bus window ruffled the dog's mane. As the dog barked a welcome at the wind's caress, his owner scratched his head and looked out at a scene she had tirelessly waited to see on a month's long road trip—the Rocky Mountain range in Banff, Canada. Inspired as I watched the serene scene of green pines and snow-white tops unfold on the Netflix documentary Expedition Happiness, Selima and Felix's journey across North America represented a bold adventure of discovering what makes us happy. Not your average German couple, the pair flew to North Carolina to buy and retrofit an old school bus to be their loft on wheels.

The process took longer than anticipated, and the pair soon ran out of days in their travel visa.[68]

With no time to spare, the couple hit the road to cross the border into Toronto, Canada, determined to arrive before the visa expired. Once in Canada, the couple drove through all the provinces, from Ontario to Yukon, wearing their childhood dreams on their sleeves as they approached the border to Alaska, hoping to cross. The border patrol let them cross the checkpoint, and while both were ecstatic, they could feel the toll on their bodies after months on end of driving and sleeping on the road. After taking in the last frontier of Alaska, the couple headed south to Mexico and were greeted by the hospitable culture of the Mexican people.

Driving lengthy distances from place to place can be exhausting, but it also allows you the flexibility to travel at your own pace. While there may be many sights to see along the road trip or within the particular town, city, or village, to get a deeper feel for a place, pick one or two on the list where you will spend most of your time. Knowing that most of the time you spend will be behind the wheel, I opt for scenic drives whenever I can, especially for lengthier drives. This may also mean taking the longer route so that you have scenic stops to take in the drive and landscape around you.

Road trips can also teach you about yourself. Each day and hour of the drive can be a test in patience, but in my

---

68 Expedition Happiness, directed by Selima Taibi, written by Selima Taibi and Felix Starck, featuring Selima Taibi and Felix Starck, aired May 4, 2017, on Netflix.

experience, these moments stick with you because of how much you tend to reflect about yourself and the people you may be with when traveling with others. There is no better time for reflection than behind wheels on an open road with limited distraction to keep our minds occupied. I happen to find stimulating scenery like mountains, coastlines, and forests stimulating for my mind. These scenes inspire time for reflection, and as such, I prefer to plan road trips which include those aspects. You may find that cityscapes and bridges are your flavor of inspiration. Whatever the case, road tripping can be a sustainable option for the environment when traveling with a group. It is also a surefire way to be more mindful while on your travels because of the focus it requires for long periods of time.

Watching Expedition Happiness reminded me of my experiences visiting a few of the same places the couple had highlighted on their road trip.[69] I remember the weightlessness I felt as the wind whipped around my hair, and I burst out in song with the music blasting, a total sense of freedom. I remember the cold in my bones fading away at the sight of the mountains in Banff, which was enhanced by my dip in the hot springs later that evening. I remember the excitement of making childhood fantasies come true when driving through the seven million acres that is the Chugach National Forest in Alaska, amazed that one place could have that much snow.

Beyond our similar experiences, I had embarked on my own road trip tour through America, for "happyness," for peace of mind, or for something in which to believe in.

---

69 Ibid.

If you wonder why I've literally spelled happyness this way, look no further than Christopher Gardner.

While on the road reflecting on my winding journey from childhood traumas, I discovered Gardner's truth to happyness, an inspiring tale. Amid his hardships as a working homeless Veteran and single father overcoming many of the negative cycles of trauma he experienced as a child, Gardner remained steadfast in his pursuit of what he phrased as happyness.[70] I realized I, too, had to overcome negative cycles of trauma from a past that imprisoned me in its grief and insecurities.

When I saw the same telltale signs in others, their unhappyness reflected like a mirror and resonated with me. The core to healing is love, as I've come to learn from others who have mastered the art of coping in an unequal world. Understanding why you do things to make yourself happy is important. Equally important is paying close attention to what you avoid or escape because they make you unhappy; this comes more easily when you are honest with yourself.

The trips I embarked on to find my truth would be for work or vacation, or a mix of both for what I call the work-cation. I felt inspired to find sustainability in my travels after watching Selima and Felix's story of condensing their trip to a year while living sustainably, efficiently, and mostly off-grid in their apartment on wheels. The one critique I would add, as I've learned myself, is to not rush through a trip across America for the sake of finding happyness quicker or for

---

70 "Biography," Chris Gardner's official website, accessed June 4, 2020.

some other profitable cause. My own journey across America took several years, made possible because of jobs, conferences, or career opportunities that took place in different states.

However, there was a time, prior to moving to our nation's capital, where I hadn't experienced much of the country outside of Florida. There was also a time where I was looking at flights abroad instead of taking the time to experience my own backyard. Even with a limited understanding of what my own country was like, I was chasing what I thought was the greener grass. In the process, I could not develop gratitude for my home country because I was always preparing my bucket list of what new overseas place was next.

Finding truth in this context is an exercise in learning yourself—and loving that person—while taking time to understand how others view you and you them. As I've come to find truth in fully embracing and loving myself, I am able to love others around the globe, and that manifests in how I am an activist for the causes I care about most. Furthermore, in taking a mindfulness moment to recognize that traveling is an immense privilege and not guaranteed, as evidenced by our recent global pandemic, I am reminded to be grateful for every country I've ever visited, including the states within my own country.

SELF-DISCOVERY ON SOLO ROAD TRIPS ACROSS AMERICA

I'd never been to Wyoming. I honestly hadn't given it much thought, and yet it was home to the first US National Park established in March 1872, covering Wyoming, Montana, and Idaho.[71]

I had already driven several hours through Colorado and was on my way to Yellowstone National Park.

Out here, there was nothing but land, mountains, and plains rife with deer, moose, and yes, even a bear.

The cars had stopped and started pulling over to the side when I saw it, a golden-brown young adult bear grazing on berries on the incline of the side of a mountain. All of a sudden, the bear looked around with its beady eyes like the black pits of fruit and sniffed the air. The next thing we visitors knew, the bear was bounding down the incline and made its way to the road. I stayed in my car, rolling my window down to capture photographs from what I hoped was a safe enough distance. The bear made one low growl, more like a yawn, as its razor-sharp, yellow-stained teeth glinted and then looked for an opening between two cars that led down another incline to the lake. Everyone stayed still in that moment, in fear and awe as we saw the bear carrying about its life and proceed to bathe in the lake below. I had not expected to see a bear this up close and personal. As I thought about it further, this had to be the first one I'd ever seen out in the wild. I knew I would never forget the experience, and as I breathed in sighing with gratitude for the wildlife, the fresh mountain air seemed to agree with my

71 "The Restless Giant," National Park Service, Yellowstone, accessed June 4, 2020.

sentiment. Yellowstone instilled a deeper appreciation for visiting national and state parks.

As my discovery journey was just beginning, I realized I had overlooked the treasures in my own backyard in search of gems I thought would exist in another country. I'm not an avid driver, as I mentioned before, but my experience in our first National Park was the truth I needed to find as I practiced gratitude for my privileges of being able to drive somewhere new. Yellowstone also spurred a series of intentional and spontaneous road-tripping both to places I had always wanted to visit and to parts of the country that remained a mystery but that I would discover were highly underrated.

When I visit the National Parks, I usually stop at small mountain towns and close-by cities. While I had never heard of these towns before, I kept an open mind and would go off exploring the main road in search of a hot meal and a hospitable atmosphere. One of my favorite simple moments on the trip to Yellowstone occurred in Thermopolis, Wyoming, when a family sitting at the table across from me in a diner invited me to eat with them. I was still on my way to Yellowstone and politely declined their offer, but we chatted for a few minutes about the area. The family's genuine desire for fellowship would stick with me for the rest of the trip.

Why hadn't I taken up their offer to eat with them? Did I have some unresolved fears of eating with strangers? Perhaps I wasn't as open-minded as I thought. Or worse, I was so caught up in getting to my destination as soon as possible that I missed out on a moment to travel slower.

SLOW TRAVEL MOVEMENT

Slow travel emphasizes taking in one's surroundings at a relaxed pace and seeing new places or cultures in a way that's less stressful, better for the environment, better for your budget, and more respective of the locals.[72]

I was curious to learn more about slow travel, knowing that my pace of traveling at an average of ten new countries every year for four years was not exactly slow. Furthermore, I had succeeded in turning some of my international trips into missions to see as much as possible while barely giving myself the room of a few extra days to do nothing. While living fast certainly has its appeal, we are missing the point when we treat travel the same way we treat our daily productive lives.

I also appreciated that the slow travel movement was inspired by the "slow food movement, which began in Italy in the 1980s as a protest against the opening of [fast food] . . . and to preserve regional cuisine, local farming, communal meals, and traditional food preparation."[73] Since then, the cultural phenomenon and practice of slower travel emerged into the Slow Movement, which spans travel, cities, food, education, living, money, and reading. "The Slow Movement aims to address the issue of time poverty through connections," and in the case of travel, this means taking the time to connect with locals and their culture, which I could have experienced had I slowed down in Thermopolis.[74]

---

72 Sarah Schlichter, "The Art of Slow Travel," Smarter Travel (blog), February 12, 2019.

73 Ibid.

74 Ibid.

AN UNSUSTAINABLE LIFESTYLE

A few months after Yellowstone, I was staring across the cliffside overlooking the Pacific Ocean on my latest road trip along the Oregon coast. The scenery reminded me of how Cheryl Strayed had lost her boot somewhere along the Pacific Crest Trail. I remember her utter frustration as she screamed and threw the other boot over a cliffside. Breathing in that frustration, she felt the emotion for a moment, let the emotion pass, and then in sheer determination, duct-taped her sandals to her feet with a plan to resolve this setback at the next trail checkpoint.[75]

I could resonate. I sighed deeply, worry-creasing my forehead as my mind flooded with work tasks in need of completion, errands back at home, and what the next thing in my life would be.

At that moment, saltwater misted my face, waking me from my reverie as it splashed the tops of rocks guarding several sea caves right beneath my feet.

Eureka—not the city in Oregon, though I was close—dawned on me. My lifestyle was unsustainable. I was simply doing and thinking too much. My mind and body were subliminally forcing me to stop with each increasing desire to escape to the open road to refill my cup. But I couldn't keep running forever. I would eventually have to deal with my responsibilities when I came back. I knew I was onto something with calling out my unsustainable life, but as I opened my eyes,

---

75   Cheryl Strayed, Wild: From Lost to Found on the Pacific Crest Trail (New York: Alfred A. Knopf, 2012).

and really opened them, my breath caught in my throat with gratitude.

The mix of ocean, cliffs, mountains, and forests was a feast for the eyes. I realized this moment embodied a nature lover's dream. As I reminisce on this trip, what's wild about that cliffside hike is it was completely unplanned.

Before taking the road trip from Boise, Idaho, to Portland at the end of a work meeting, I had already done a fair amount of research, including several nature bloggers' suggestions for Oregon. I could tell that many of these nature hikers and bloggers lived for the off-beaten paths and risk-taking adventures to include climbing rocks in the middle of the Pacific.

While several bloggers had shared these paths with the world, I decided there are paths that should remain solely the path of the hiker, understanding the beauty in leaving a place to be discovered by others who set out on their own respective pilgrimages. While I won't share this exact oceanside hike, nor can I, for I did not take my phone with me to drop a pin in the location, I hope you'll discover your own eureka moments on paths like this one.

The scenery and solitude of these road trips were immensely therapeutic. They offered a reprieve from my unsustainable lifestyle and forced me to slow down or put away whatever obligations may exist back home, back at work, or in the back of my mind. But to sustain them, I would need to learn how to implement some of these practices back home.

MASLOW'S HIERARCHY OF NEEDS

Happyness was abundant while on my travels, but a fleeting memory never reaching far enough into my daily reality to be sustainable. It was like a drug, whereas my level of happyness decreased, so increased my desire to go somewhere new and escape what I considered to be a suffocating life. Having heard of Maslow's Hierarchy of Needs, developed by psychologist Abraham Maslow in 1943, I wanted to explore the concept of finding happyness and fulfillment in my life.[76]

Maslow's Hierarchy of Needs is a theory of motivation based on five categories of human needs.[77] Starting at the bottom, needs start at the physiological to include food, shelter, and sleep. Next is safety and security. Then love and belonging to self-esteem. At the top is self-actualization.

When we travel, these same needs come into play. In some cases, our awareness of them heightens because we are in unfamiliar territory and can't autopilot our way to self-actualization. Traveling itself can be a form of self-actualization though our ability to curate and participate in deep, meaningful travel experiences may be limited if we haven't personally met the other levels. In this instance, and in my personal experience, travel shifted from self-actualization to more of an escape from addressing my needs or from the pain associated with being denied access to these needs either through systemic barriers or personal unhealthy relationships.

---

76 Pursuit of Happiness, Inc., "Abraham Maslow," accessed June 5, 2020.

77 Ibid.

I often felt like I was bouncing up and down levels, sometimes straddling multiple levels when trying to bite off more than I could chew, or perhaps I was approaching the whole thing wrong. Later on, Maslow clarified that satisfying needs on one level was not "all-or-none" and that his earlier statements might have falsely characterized that a need must be satisfied at 100 percent before the next need can be addressed.[78] Maslow postured that the order of needs might depend on external circumstances or individual differences as some individuals may prioritize self-esteem over love or creative fulfillment over basic needs.

How many of you have been guilty of letting a passion project take up your whole day, forgetting about sleep while crunching down on snacks from the corner store?

I must admit, I am guilty of this myself. In my journey toward finding myself, I knew balancing my respective needs would be important to my self-care.

The needs are characterized as deficit and growth. The deficit needs refer to the four lower levels of Maslow's Hierarchy, and indicate a lack of something, while growth needs stem from one's desire to grow. Progress to address the needs is disrupted by failures to meet the lower levels, and in particular, the physiological ones like sleep and food.

The truth is, sometimes we won't be able to make it to the top of the hierarchy and stay there. Doing so can shield us too often from the reality that most face, cause us to get too

---

78 Ibid.

comfortable in our surroundings, and breed ignorance or disdain for others who haven't made it as high up the pyramid. This is apparent even in how the needs are characterized as deficiency versus growth needs. The first four levels of the pyramid are thought of as deficiency needs, while the very top is considered a growth need. Deficiencies exist where there is deprivation or a lack of access and motivates people to act the longer they remain unmet. During your travels, it can be good to make room to address the lower needs immediately or to have a plan for how they'll be addressed. The longer I've been on the road, the more I've valued this level of preparation, to the point where I'll have my go-to items on hand in my backpack or on my person.

But I posit that Maslow's Hierarchy is not so much a pyramid of levels to climb so much as it is an entire mountain range filled with peaks and valleys. We have all seen examples of what climbing the ladder can proverbially look like for our respective lives, but how many of us have thought about what the climb or hike down looks like? Can we make that descent into the valley of a life less painful and prepare for it the same way we prepare ourselves to climb the ladder? Not doing so leads to a perpetual state of escaping or running away, as I soon came to find. I also knew there was a lot I should be grateful for, and to do that due diligence, I needed to get to a place where I could more easily appreciate the peaks in life while making it through the valleys.

WHY ESCAPING THROUGH TRAVEL IS NOT SUSTAINABLE

According to a Psychology Today article written by Dr. Jeremy Sherman, a bio-philosopher and social science researcher, there are various coping strategies that humans, either subconsciously or consciously, employ: face-it and escapist.[79]

1. Face-it strategies provide calm strength to face reality more realistically.
2. Escapist strategies encourage ignoring the aspects of our reality that cause the most stress or anxiety. [80]

I had previously mentioned addictions as distracting our progress from addressing needs. Because of this, they can be viewed as escapist because they alter our outlook and can make it easy to ignore our reality, often with the intent to achieve self-actualization quicker. When we lean into escapist strategies, we rob ourselves of the problem-solving skills and rationale we need to make sound judgments not only in life but in our travels.

MINDFUL PRACTICES IN TRAVEL

Knowing I was exhibiting escapist strategies, I went back to my Indian roots for the concepts of yoga and mindfulness. Mindfulness, according to Bhavani, my first yoga instructor from India, is taking the time to immerse yourself in the present moment. Mindfulness can include listening to all

---

79 Jeremy Sherman, "Face-it Versus Escapist Coping Strategies," Psychology Today, April 10, 2017.

80 Ibid.

of the sounds in your vicinity and picking them out one by one. Perhaps the most important to listen to is the sound of your own breathing.

Are your breaths shallow and labored, or long and measured?

Bhavani's teachings, while rooted in our Indian culture, naturally piqued my curiosity as I started paying closer attention to the environment and its connection to my life. I had to separate the things that were naturally on my mind due to worrying about them and replace them with the magic that is staying curious about the environment.

My Indian Canadian cousin Sonika appreciates a different kind of winding road on her travels: one she can walk along. For her, an ideal vacation includes the art of flaneur outside and growing up in Canada, she learned the French term flaneur means to enjoy a walk without purpose.

I could see how walking around a city or on a nature path could be mindful, and it reminded me of the concept of forest bathing, which I had read about from an eco-blogger. Josephine Becker's encouragement to spend more time outdoors, as outlined in her support for an eco-friendly lifestyle, applies to the principles behind meditation.[81] Josephine learned about forest bathing on her outdoor adventures. Forest bathing, a form of deep meditation in nature, is thought to have originated in Japan in the 1980s.[82] Japanese government officials conducted research to discern what, if any, physical

---

81 Kelly Green, "What I Learnt Forest Bathing," Eco-Age, May 15, 2019.

82 Ibid.

and mental health benefits would arise from forest bathing and found extensive positive results.[83]

Whether it's flaneur or forest bathing, both kinds of experiences encourage us to travel slower. Perhaps I want to stay in a specific place to learn more about the culture and locals. Giving ourselves the time to fully reflect on and understand a place and its people, knowing that time builds trust and understanding, can be an incredibly meaningful way to approach travel. But if you don't know and trust yourself first, then it will be hard to trust others and their intentions.

Mindfulness can be viewed as the opposite of escapism, as it is simply reflecting on what your life is as of this moment. For people who are escaping, facing, or even the mere act of thinking about one's reality may be too terrifying or depressing. Escaping is a "way of attempting to make negative feelings dissipate without working through the steps to find relief in a more permanent mental resolution."[84] Escapism, on the other hand, provides a false sense of relief, a quick fix, and a placebo. Similar to my travels, I would find myself happy in the moment, in the journey from point A in my hometown to point B and C in another state or country with so many possibilities and endless opportunities to distract myself from what was hurting or bothering me most. I didn't realize just how much I was practicing escapism until I came back from a trip, and not even two days later, I felt the same stress and disappointment I felt days before my trip.

---

83   Ibid.

84   Sherman, "Face-it Versus Escapist Coping Strategies."

For a long time, I used escapist strategies in planning my trips and when on the road. When I started looking at travel as a way to run away from issues I might be facing or that give me a lot of stress, I knew I was doing a disservice to being grateful for the privilege that traveling affords.

So here I was back at the starting point of how to translate the happyness I experienced on my travels to my life back home. And I realized the more I asked that question, the more intentional I was with my reflections from my trips. Beyond wander-lusting and daydreaming of faraway lands, I was replicating the same practices I had discovered and grown to love about my experiences abroad, discovering the hidden gems of each city, town, or community.

The hard work of reflecting on our happiest moments is something we either don't make time for or realize it requires a consistent practice of gratitude. Perhaps we are going through a stormy season, we've lost someone, our relationships are unsatisfying, our work is whittling us down until that initial fire ablaze has been burned out.

I had to learn to create what I loved about travel here at home for those moments I can't physically go anywhere.

I started finding peace and pleasure out of the mundane because I was thankful for the time to just walk around without any pressures and the ability to see everything around me. It took a while for me to quiet the noise in my mind, but the longer I walked, the more it helped.

Once I was able to experience this in the simplicity of my backyard, it empowered me to level up my travel experiences even more. What's important is that your own remedy be just as simple. Perhaps it's not yoga because all those movements are just too much, but whatever you choose as your process, it is yours alone and isn't comparable to others', so you can stop comparing now. You are in control of what you are, and that includes the things you need to be more mindful so you can resource and love yourself better.

I was able to focus because I knew I had limited time, and I wanted to get what I could out of this break I had created for myself. To help you, I've included an exercise I often practice while on my thought walks. I incorporate each level of Maslow's Hierarchy of Needs so that you can practice navigating through the peaks and valleys of the hierarchy in your approach to happiness as a hike and not simply a climb.

Thought Walk: A Mindfulness Exercise Based on Maslow's Hierarchy

Love and Belonging Questions	
Questions	**Your answer**
What do you see and hear around you as you're walking?	
What is around you?	
What is making the noises you hear?	

Mindful Exercise

Take a moment to appreciate all that you see and hear. You can press your feet into the Earth. If you can find an open field or a sandy beach to do this in while barefoot, it will empower you while feeding your connection with the environment.

Begin to feel your body as you take each step and as you shorten or lengthen each stride.

Esteem Questions

Questions	Your answer
Are thoughts invading your mind?	
How do you feel about yourself?	

Mindful Exercise

If you find you are distracted, create a folder in your mind of where you'll place that thought. Right now you're on your walk and the walk is sacred and valuable time you've created for yourself as a priority.

Physiological & Safety Needs Questions

Questions	Your answer
If you find your walk is taking longer than expected, am I avoiding confrontation or delaying addressing the worry or distraction I placed in that folder in my mind?	
If you find you physically don't feel optimal ask yourself what have you eaten today? How much water have you consumed?	
Did you do what was required to support your physical wellbeing?	

BEYOND POST-TRAVEL DEPRESSION OR BLUES

When talking with my Mexican Indigenous friend Oscar, who had recently taken a trip to his ancestral homeland in Mexico, we discussed the realities of post-travel depression after returning home.

Post-travel depression leaves behind an immense longing for life on the road and the sense of loss at not being able to do that because other priorities in life come to the forefront. Time passes, and the feelings linger as you reminisce on those photos or journal entries. While I knew I might not be happy today, all I could do was move forward and remain confident that I would be able to experience the privilege of traveling once more.

Another world traveler, Tomislav, speaks about the realities of post travel depression. You could go back to the security of your old lifestyle, your same friends talking about the same things, and maybe even get your old job back, but some part of you will miss the traveler version of you, with the intensity you felt wherever you were going, unsure of what gems the next adventure would hold. He suggests that one can hit the road again and continue the nomadic lifestyle, but after a while, that too will reveal something missing in the sense of a home or belonging to a community. "There's a sadness that comes with the friendships you make on the road, which, while intense, will be mostly short-lived."[85] Much to my chagrin, he offers up a middle path of mixing the two where you still carry that level of intensity you had as a world traveler in your own country by walking streets you've never been on before, talking with people on the street you've never spoken to or might not have spoken to otherwise, cultivating a new hobby or job that better suits whom you've become instead of whom you were, writing a book about said travels, or giving a TEDxTalk.[86] His point is, the world is open to you if you decide to explore it with the same level of intensity you had when you were soaking in all the new and unknown things on your trips to various countries or states.

---

85 Tomislav Perko, "How to travel the world with almost no money," filmed February 2015 at TEDxTUHH, Hamburg University of Technology, Hamburg, Germany, video.

86 Ibid.

In prioritizing sustainable happyness, I had to come to the realization that I was letting external forces dictate the way I felt and that it was robbing me of the freedom to choose my own coping strategy. Dr. Sherman says that when we have the freedom to choose and face what is true, we are happier and healthier company for others.[87]

LIVING VICARIOUSLY THROUGH MEMORIES
Driving with the window down in the middle of nowhere with my thoughts and my freedom are what I reflect on when I reminisce on these happy moments in my life. There is always an origin and a destination, but I have learned to embrace the journey along the way, knowing this part would soon be over.

By practicing gratitude for walking along paths in my own backyard, I was able to best post travel blues and be grateful for my surrounding environment. In practicing gratitude, I was also able to reflect on all that I had experienced thus far, and I realized that sharing my travel stories with the world reenergized me.

You caught me.

I'm definitely leveraging this book to relive some of my favorite moments and live vicariously through others while understanding the bigger picture of why I travel.

---

87   Sherman, "Face-it Versus Escapist Coping Strategies."

When I am grateful for these moments on the road trips I've been privileged to take, I feel happier. A smile also plays on my lips as I look around at the current state of travel in the wake of a global pandemic and realize others are finally experiencing what I had been doing for years.

The solitude offered from being in your car affords a certain level of safety and autonomy in designing your own journey and making stops as needed along the way. With you in control of your journey and destination, road trips can be designed with as much or little contact with others based on your comfort level. As we learned, driving in a car is not more sustainable than flying in a plane unless you fill all your seats. One option to make the journey more comfortable for you and family or friends, is to use an RV or trailer attached to your car for your camping and driving needs. RVs can be cost and energy-efficient, operating as a house on wheels, while also providing a true reprieve from the hustle and bustle of the modern, urban world. Road trips also provide an opportunity to explore a slower pace of life consistent with the slow travel movement.

In driving through America, I learned how to be more strategic about the stops I took as my in-between experiences from origin to destination. The question to ask yourself is whether you are someone who is prepared for the road or if you would rather visit a place through a more convenient way, say flying, to eliminate the inconvenience of burning time on the road. What I found is that driving solo and flying had a similar carbon footprint. To offset the carbon footprint while driving, one would need to travel with a companion, which also makes for a more interesting road trip.

Beyond mindfulness for the environment is mindfulness for yourself while on these trips. Learning how to practice gratitude while adapting to each new situation presented by visiting a new state is what you can discover as a road tripper.

While finding truth represents the first mindset on a journey toward sustainability, putting into action the practices discussed in this chapter will heighten your appreciation for traveling. Of course, equally important is maintaining an open mind so as to be able to appreciate what another country has to offer.

CHAPTER 6

PRE-CLIMATE AND CLIMATE CHANGES

——

IN THE EYE OF THE STORM

The smell of new books, the wax on the floor, the grandeur of opening classroom doors like portals to new worlds of knowledge and understanding greeted me upon starting high school.

Little did I know that the excitement I felt from starting high school would be cut short.

Not even two weeks after starting, we heard an announcement that school would be closed for the rest of the week.

A few of you might assume the cancelation of classes would be exciting. For the other students and me, this immediately reminded us of the severity that comes with hurricane season in Florida. This was spurred on as our history teacher reminisced on her experience with Hurricane Andrew in the early 1990s. Like Hurricane Andrew, the hurricane approaching us boasted the highest ranking, a category five, and there was at least one more tropical storm forming in the Atlantic not too far away.

What we didn't know at the time was that we would get hit with not one but three devastating category four and five hurricanes that would have us all out of school for a month as we navigated flooded towns and destroyed property, including my mother's van. Offering a helping hand in my community wasn't new to me. In the aftermath of the hurricane, I went out right after the storms cleared to remove debris, bring food and water to people, and assist organizations providing relief.

Reflecting on my personal experiences during hurricane season, I think about how the destruction left in their wake is worsening. Recently, we've seen these storms ravage the island territories of Puerto Rico and US Virgin Islands, as well as our neighbors in the Bahamas. For me, natural disasters were only getting worse and more aggressive. I was curious as to how much human activities contributed to this.

According to Yale Climate Connections, a nonpartisan, multimedia service that does broadcast radio programming and original web-based reporting, commentary, and analysis on the issues of climate change, the warmer water temperatures result in more available heat energy and therefore a higher likelihood for tropic cyclones to develop.[88] As we continue to consume and release greenhouse gases from our behaviors,

---

88 Jeff Berardelli, "How climate change is making hurricanes more dangerous," Yale Climate Connections, accessed May 5, 2020.

we warm our planet.[89] We'll also need to expect tropical and hurricane activity to increase as well, including their severity.

It's easy to see how hurricane activity is at its most severe when Puerto Rico is still recovering from one of the deadliest hurricanes in their history. In response to the devastation they faced with their economy following this natural disaster, I decided to take a work trip to the US territory.

* * *

I shaded my eyes overlooking a warm midday sun from my hotel balcony, where the waves were crashing against the caramel sanded shoreline to my right. "Bienvenida senorita, quieres una botella de agua?" the hotel host said. "Por su puesto, gracias para su hospitalidad," I replied, slightly self-conscious of my Spanish. Unbothered and hospitably cheerful, the host handed me a refreshingly cold bottle of water, and I responded with a bashful smile of appreciation. I was in Puerto Rico for a work trip nearly two years after the devastation of Hurricane Maria in September 2017. I had never been to Puerto Rico, but I knew Spanish and wanted to try my hand at getting around Old San Juan. I had flown in on a Sunday before a multi-day work conference on senior leadership strategies for state and territorial health agencies and didn't have any major work responsibilities that day, so I took advantage of the time to explore the barrio (colloquial Spanish term for neighborhood). Strolling on a warm Sunday afternoon, the scene couldn't have been more picturesque,

---

89 Ibid.

the sea a calm blue presence of rhythmic waves as the palms were caressed by a light breeze.

I couldn't imagine a hurricane within miles of this place, and yet Hurricane Maria's devastation had resulted in an unknown death count, the deadliest event for Puerto Rico in a century, and the largest disaster medical response and housing operation in America's history.[90] A year ago, it would have been impossible to go to Puerto Rico, not to mention a burden on the current systems in place because anyone visiting would need resources such as food, water, electricity, and housing, which would be used and taken away from others in dire need, still waiting for recovery on the stoop of their now destroyed porches. No, the territory needed time to recover and needed to save its resources to rebuild.

As I do with most of my trips, I did some light internet searching and reached out to friends who had been to Puerto Rico for their recommendations before traversing the calles—streets—of Old San Juan. The tragic fact was that many of those restaurants or businesses were long closed, which was no more sobering than at the moment that I was staring down at my phone's Google Maps and looking back up at the building that was now abandoned and painted with a graffiti message of esperanza (hope) across an image of a flag of Puerto Rico. During my few hours exploring, I was especially mindful of how I was spending my dollar and took time to visit family-owned restaurants, food truck cafes, and street vendors, with the understanding that I was

---

90 Puerto Rico One Year After Hurricane Maria (New York: Center for Puerto Rican Studies, The City University of New York, October 2018).

directly supporting the local Boricuas, a common term for Puerto Ricans. While my Spanish was a little rusty from lack of speaking, the local people were happy to converse with someone willing to try, which in turn only increased my enthusiasm and confidence to strike up a conversation with a local whenever and wherever I could.

There are many solid strategies and practices that make my personal travel experience in Puerto Rico worth emulating, but many of those were unknown to me at the time. Since then, I've taken time to think about what happened while I was there, and in my reflection, understand that I was learning about the way of life of the Boricuas and grateful for their willingness to open up to me with the familiar underpinnings of their rich Taíno-based culture. Taínos are the indigenous mixed-race people of Puerto Rico who populated most of the Caribbean and adjacent islands during the Pre-Colombian era before the arrival of the Spaniards.[91]

According to the Center for Puerto Rican Studies at the City University of New York, even a year later, Puerto Rico still faced an unstable electric grid, infrastructure issues, the largest municipal bankruptcy in history, 265 school closures, small businesses with surmounting financial losses, and death rates higher than birth rates for the first time in the island territory's history.[92]

---

91 Encyclopedia Britannica Online, s.v. "Taino," accessed September 3, 2020.

92 Puerto Rico One Year After Hurricane Maria, Center for Puerto Rican Studies, The City University of New York.

The Puerto Rico Planning Board and other survey data from public/private entities estimate the damages cost anywhere between forty-three and ninety-five billion.[93] This sobering knowledge humbled me as I engaged with Boricuas across the island. And while it shouldn't take a tragedy or devastation for us to stop taking for granted the ability to travel to other places, sometimes it's exactly what compels us to reflect on the privilege of visiting a place.

The emotional turmoil a hurricane invokes also plays out in one of my favorite movies, *Day After Tomorrow*, which is eerily more relevant today than when it was first released coincidentally the same year as the onslaught of hurricanes I faced in high school. One of the key themes that the movie speaks to is the lack of preparation for climate change. The scene opens up with climate scientist Jack Hall speaking with a colleague who works for the government on what models they have prepared in anticipation of the looming global natural disaster.[94]

Terry Rapson: "There are no forecast models remotely capable of plotting this scenario—except yours."

Jack Hall (climate scientist): "My model is a reconstruction of a prehistoric climate shift. It's not a forecast model."

---

93 Ibid.

94 Day After Tomorrow, directed by Roland Emmerich (Los Angeles, CA: 20th Century Studios, Inc., 2004), film.

Terry Rapson: "It's the closest thing we have. Nothing like this has ever happened before."[95]

As Terry closes that dialogue with the chilling reality that they are dealing with an unprecedented storm, it reminds me of our recent unprecedented global pandemic, novel coronavirus or COVID-19. I also think about how many times we've experienced unprecedented natural disasters in the last few years, including worsening hurricanes and wildfires across the globe.

In *Day After Tomorrow*, with each passing minute of the film, the weather events worsen. The vice president remains skeptical of the severity of the weather changes until it's too late to save Americans in the northern part of the country. This time Day After Tomorrow dialogue is between the Vice President and a government official who is working with Jack Hall.

Vice President Becker: "I don't accept that abandoning half the country is necessary."

Tom: "Maybe if you would have listened to him sooner, it wouldn't be."

Vice President Becker: "Oh bulls***. It's easy for him to suggest this plan, he's safely here [and privileged] in Washington."

---

95 Ibid.

Tom: "His son is in Manhattan. I just thought you should know . . . before questioning his motives."[96]

What scientists had predicted to occur in the next several decades unfolded in Day After Tomorrow within a couple of days, depicting how unprepared the country was to mitigate the event. I remember the surreal feeling of watching the main disaster manifest in NASA's aerial view of super hurricane storms covering most of the planet. I found it interesting how those astronauts depicted in space while playing their part to transmit the images of the Earth and other satellite data were far removed from the dangers and realities Earth was facing at that moment.

As I reminisced on the scene with the vice president, I thought how closely art imitates life as I fast forward to the present day and remain disgruntled that there are politicians who still debate whether climate change is real.

OUR HOUSE IS ON FIRE

Reality hit when our own backyard caught on fire during a global pandemic.

The heat that bears down from the firestorms on the west coast of America moves so fast that to survive, people must leave their homes immediately. The resulting aftermath

---

96 Ibid.

includes displacement from homes, hazardous smoke in the air, and death.[97]

I first became more attuned to the realities of climate change in a college class on the social impact of climate change. I learned that some of the devastation previewed in Day After Tomorrow's opening sequence of glaciers breaking off and sea levels rising was actually occurring at a rapid pace in our poles.

I decided to witness and document firsthand how this was happening in our arctic regions, so I looked for opportunities to travel to places like Iceland and Alaska. My foray into Alaska awakened a fascination and sense of protection for natural resources and beauty as I discovered much more than a cooler climate. When I learned about what was happening to the coastal islands of Alaska, it made me that much more passionate about being part of the solution to the climate change impacts facing our polar regions and their ripple effects on the rest of the world. I saw wildlife in danger of going extinct, I heard the thunder of glaciers breaking apart and melting, and I discovered the impact it had on people's livelihoods by disrupting hunting and gathering.

According to NASA's satellites, Greenland and Antarctica's ice sheets and glaciers have been shrinking in size.[98] When the ice melts or breaks off, the water flows into the ocean

97 Blacki Migliozzi, Scott Reinhard, Nadja Popovich, Tim Wallace, and Allison McCann, "Record Wildfires on the West Coast Are Capping a Disastrous Decade," New York Times, September 24, 2020.

98 NASA "Understanding Sea Level," NASA, accessed May 5, 2020.

resulting in rising sea levels. If all glaciers and known ice sheets melted, NASA estimates that the global sea level would rise by more than 195 feet or sixty meters, which would wipe out most places below sea level.[99] As oceans continue to fill with broken ice sheets and pieces from nearby glaciers, sea levels also rise. These glacial fragments then reflect and absorb the sun's warmth, thus warming the oceans beneath them even more than if they had not melted.[100]

With all this devastation at our door and science that we are either too skeptical of or which makes us depressingly anxious about our future, what's the takeaway, especially as a traveler navigating or wishing to navigate some of these places that are impacted the hardest from changes to the climate?

Do we stop visiting them and consequently impact our ability to fuel their economy via tourism? Do we visit them in haste, knowing they will soon be gone, and accept with resignation that this is our reality? Or rather, is there some way we can leave a positive impact behind when we visit?

Skeptics believe that global warming is not imminent and will take a while for humanity to feel its impact. They divert attention and resources to combatting this looming threat by focusing on what they consider to be more pressing global issues.

---

99 Ibid.

100 Ibid.

They will say, "You don't know the way the world works. This is not the priority and can be the next generation's problem to fix."

Well, the next generation is here and knocking. Like Greta Thunberg exclaimed to buttoned-up professionals at the 2019 UN Climate Action Summit after a months-long journey across the Atlantic, "How dare you . . . if you fail us, we will never forgive you."[101]

Global warming can have resounding impacts like an ice age as the warming can trigger a cooling trend for the Earth. This inherently has costs for the infrastructures we have in place that were not designed to withstand this kind of environmental stressor or were not tested with this scenario in mind. The economic, architectural, educational, workforce, and healthcare infrastructures have already shown how we've stressed them to their breaking point amid the COVID-19 global pandemic.

How prepared are we if a global natural disaster strikes like COVID-19?

I don't feel so optimistic as I contend with the reality that federal funding and resources are minimal due to decisions made by skeptical leaders who question the potential threat of climate impacts.

---

101 Greta Thunberg, "Greta Thunberg blasts world leaders: We will never forgive you" CBC News, streamed live on September 23, 2019, YouTube video, 4:28.

I think about how our government responds to emergencies we should know about, but do not prepare for—a scramble to pass emergency supplemental funding overnight. We run the risk of being wholly unprepared to deal with the consequences, especially if such a disaster wipes out our power grids, similar to Puerto Rico's challenges after Hurricane Maria. What keeps me up at night is how we would manage without electricity or the internet during a global disaster.

What is our plan for connecting when we have no power?

While this was commonplace for us to prepare for in Florida based on past experience with category five hurricanes, not everyone could afford or implement such a plan. Backup generators worked for a time, but most of us would go out and connect with those in our neighborhood to keep ourselves safe, resourced, and surviving until the power returned, which could take as long as a week or more. We were usually well-stocked with nonperishables, canned goods, and plenty of candles to go around, but this became more difficult if one's house or car sustained significant damages; insurance always took a complicated and long time to address these.

I think if you don't take away anything else, I encourage you to face the reality that climate change is our problem to address as humans. One only has to look at the copious examples of natural disasters from weather-related events, which devastate our cities and countries around the globe.

Scientists have been and continue to document our pre-climate and climate changes for decades, and the trend toward warming and an unsustainable planet continues to increase.

Now that you know the truth, will you do something about this existential threat to our planet?

To speak metaphorically and literally, we are in the eye of the storm, and the worst is yet to come. Are we going to put out the fires in our homes or let them burn until we have nothing left?

PART III

OPEN-
MINDEDNESS

*You are not a tourist. You are now
part of the community.*

—BLOW RASTA, COMUNA TRECE (COMMUNITY
13), TOUR GUIDE FROM MEDELLIN, COLOMBIA

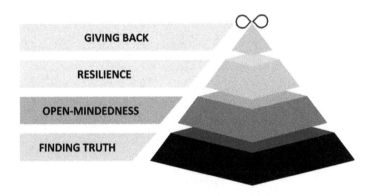

Open-Mindedness encourages us to explore the world beyond our comfort zones. While exploring, we should listen for understanding while we relate to and connect with cultures around the world. We should remain open to different types of travel experiences, including those that are better for our planet.

CHAPTER 7

THE UNIVERSAL LANGUAGE OF A GLOBAL COMMUNITY

———

"Eefoolkee," our tour guide, Ali, said with a guttural Arabic accent, his eyes twinkling from behind his thick blue headscarf, wrapped tight.

"And what does that mean?" said a young woman from Malaga, Spain, while pausing to catch her breath as our tour group crested one of the tallest sand dunes near our camp in the Sahara Desert.

"It means good or beautiful," he said as he pointed up to the sky filled with millions of stars and galaxies signaling the night.

The moon was half full as if someone sliced the first half of it off, and its muted luminescence played tricks on the eyes so that as I looked out over the Sahara Desert, it looked as if the dunes were moving like waves. I fell in love with the desert right then and there.

LOVE LANGUAGES IN THE AFRICAN DESERT

The Berbers of Morocco live a simple life full of gratitude and love for the resources the desert provides. They believe the magic and allure of the desert can make us all fall in love with the earth and their culture, just as they fall in love with ours.

Camping outdoors in the desert, one can easily be dissatisfied with the accommodations. We were exposed to the elements, coarse blankets, and mattresses dusted with a fine layer of sand while dodging camel dung on the way to the outhouse. Several of the group slept in tents circling the campfire while a few others, myself included, slept next to the fire pit to warm up due to the near-freezing temperatures at night. The humility and community we felt among our Berber tour guides were part of the experience. As a result, we were more open-minded at the top of that sand dune looking out over the desert than when we began our camelback journey into the sea of dunes. A love of nature was the first language our Berber tour guides taught us that evening.

Next, they shared a traditional Berber style dinner of couscous mixed with carrots, peppers, onions, and chicken, while also including vegetarian options, and animatedly spoke about the night's festivities to come. A group of us gathered around the fire pit as the local guides stoked the fire and began to take out their instruments. Less than five minutes later, my father danced around the campfire to the sound of rhythmic drumming and singing, a cacophony of sights and sounds. A love of music and dance was the second language they taught us.

Beyond their desert culture and music, what's notable about the Moroccan Berbers was their openness to learning from others around the world, starting with spoken languages. While speaking in English and Spanish with our tour guides, I learned that many of them hadn't received beyond the equivalent of a third-grade education due to the lack of resources in funding and teachers who were unable to journey out to the desert towns. The guides didn't let that deter them as each of them remained hopeful they could expand their education by learning phrases or entire languages. For our guides, tourism was a means by which they could make a decent living. "The world is our teacher," Ali stated, as he marveled at how much he had learned from us as visitors. A love of other cultures was the third language our Berber tour guides taught us.

When I think about this memory and others like it, I realize that not everyone would be open-minded to spend a night outdoors in the desert. But I wouldn't trade the experience for anything, as that night in the Sahara is easily one of the best nights of my life.

In thinking about our increasingly globalized world, there are several cultural elements that bring us closer together and make up the framework for a common ground, a common language. We can speak the same languages, listen to similar music, and collectively appreciate the authentic food of a country as we learn about each other's cultural norms.

These shared experiences can make the world a smaller place.

THE NO-ENGLISH RULE

Of course, you can pick up habits from our Berber friends and learn the languages of the countries you visit.

Finding himself in an Italian restaurant in Paris, Scott Young was chatting it up with an Irishman named Benny Lewis, a polyglot or someone who knows multiple languages. Scott was inspired by Lewis' accomplishment of becoming fluent in a language in three months and his bold approach to "start speaking from the very first day."[102] Scott had been worried about saying the wrong things and embarrassed by his insufficient vocabulary, yet now he had met someone who was "fearlessly div[ing] into conversations" with strangers abroad.[103]

As Scott and his roommate thought of taking time to travel the world, they created a project called "The Year Without English," where they would travel to four countries for three months each and plan to not speak English from the first day to include anyone they met and with each other.[104] Their time was spent learning from a tutor, studying at home, and spending the rest of the time talking with newfound friends, ordering at restaurants, and enjoying the country. Traveling across Spain, Brazil, China, and South Korea,

102 Scott Young, Ultralearning (New York: HarperCollins Publishers, 2019), 5–9, 17–19.

103 Ibid.

104 Ibid.

they soon came to learn that Asian languages were difficult, and "their No-English rule" started to become a challenge to enforce while also navigating these unfamiliar environments.[105]Nonetheless, at the "end of [that] year, [they] could say [they] spoke four new languages."[106] What Scott came to learn is that in the space of linguistic accomplishments, knowing multiple languages after quick immersions wasn't as rare as he initially thought as he soon learned about whole professions and communities of travelers who go from "tourist visa to tourist visa, mastering new languages."[107]

Outside of the discipline, it requires to speak another language, this is another example of openness to another culture through the willingness to learn about the people through their language and communicate with them in a way they may be able to easily understand or prefer.

NONVIOLENT COMMUNICATION

Beyond communicating in the primary language of a country you're visiting, you can also adopt other means of communicating authentically, such as nonviolent communication (NVC).

"NVC is founded on language and communication skills that strengthen our ability to remain human . . . under trying conditions and [reminds] us about . . . how we humans relate

---

105 Ibid.

106 Ibid.

107 Ibid.

to one another. NVC guides us in reframing how we express ourselves and hear others."[108]

For example, when we first experience the greeting of a kiss on both cheeks, we may feel compelled to back away out of habit or as an automatic reaction to something we are not comfortable with or do not understand completely. NVC postures that our "response should be based on our awareness of what we are perceiving, feeling, and wanting. [Once] we express ourselves with honesty, we can pay others the same respectful and empathetic attention."[109]

NVC can also be used to de-escalate disagreements or arguments with others as its principles are designed to replace patterns of behavior rooted in defensiveness, withdrawal or avoidance, violent reaction, and judgment. The NVC process clarifies what is "observed, felt, and needed rather than on diagnosing and judging" a situation.[110]

Open-mindedness helps you navigate your interactions with others, while NVC gives us a framework of how to posture ourselves to listen first, observe our own feelings and needs, and then speak.

---

108 "What is Nonviolent Communication," The Center for Nonviolent Communication, accessed May 5, 2020.

109 Ibid.

110 Ibid.

NVC PROCESS EXERCISE [111]

	Question	Your answer
Observations	What do you observe that others are saying or doing that either enriches or does not enrich your life? Then articulate what you do and do not like.	
Feelings	State how you feel when you observe this action to include whether you are hurt, frustrated, scared, overjoyed.	
Needs	State what needs of yours are connected to the feelings you have identified so that you are clear and honest.	
Requests	Follow-up with a specific request of the other person and remain open of their request.	

NVC uses an infinity symbol to represent their continual cycle of listening with empathy and expressing feelings with honesty. I interpret their use of infinity, similar to my formula, as a method for sustainable communication.

NVC provides us an opportunity to understand another's perspective even if we don't agree. Another example of this could be how we engage in a local street market. The locals may have a certain method for how each person is to walk through the market and make their selection of goods. This may include pointing out which goods or products we like versus touching and observing them for ourselves. If we respond out of impatience at the speed with which the locals walk through the market or touch items without observing their practices, it can send a message of disrespect or disregard for their cultural norms. In turn, this can spur additional reactions of disdain or critique from the locals.

---

111 Ibid.

You know what they say about Americans. This is a thought that I will often revisit when thinking about the impressions I'm leaving behind. My behaviors can set the tone for how others in a new country may perceive our culture, and it has the power to perpetuate stereotypes and turn people off from engaging us further. One example is the perception that Americans are loud wherever we go. In Japan, rules on public transportation require silence out of mutual respect for another passenger's personal and mental space. By not paying attention and carrying on like we are back home, we continue to perpetuate that thinking.

Similarly, if you share a story about another country, you are saying something about that place that you want others to take away and are using your platform to promote that particular aspect of the culture on your travels.

One example of this can include making comparisons with other countries. You might find yourself either thinking or stating to others how the streets of one country are better than another. It is important to engage in communications and practices that promote acceptance and connection with a place versus opposition or judgment. This is especially true if we wish to invite meaningful and authentic experiences with the locals.

Of course, there are times we may project our own unhappyness in our dissatisfaction or impatience with each new place. However, the more you dig deep within yourself to find the truth of what makes you happy, the better positioned you will be to apply the practices of NVC with an open mind to others' experiences. NVC can help us understand how a place impacts others' worldview. And once you've experienced one perspective, don't stop there in your quest. Keep digging to learn as much as you can from others in that country. They may begin to change your mind about what preconceived notions you had either about the culture or about life.

AN ACTIVIST'S RAP

Another form of communication that can take the form of artistic or verbal expression is music. While many genres have defied borders, the musical genre I focus on is rap and hip-hop for its use in activism and resistance against authority.[112]

For African Americans, they have come to be Americans not by choice but by the ruthlessly forced migration of their ancestors.

America's brand of slavery stripped African culture away, starting with their names, and then their semblance of the community by separating families time and again. Additional restrictions included cultural traditions, beliefs, and practices. Over time, these have been molded based on each generation's unique experiences and blended with the White European culture of the time.

African American culture developed separately from mainstream America due to racial discrimination and slave

---

112 Jeff Chang, "It's a Hip-Hop World," Foreign Policy, The Slate Group, October 12, 2009.

descendants' desire to create and maintain their own set of traditions.

These new traditions have now had a significant impact on not only the same mainstream American culture but also that of the world. One cultural phenomenon of the African American experience, which led to a redefining and reclaiming of their place in America, is the creation of hip-hop.[113]

Hip-hop has been transcending borders for decades. There are so many examples of variations of hip-hop around the world, and while each is unique in their own national flavor, they keep true to the principles of the art form in that they unite young people around the world to share a vital progressive agenda which challenges the status quo.

The African American community created hip-hop in the 1970s in the Bronx, New York, as "one of the world's most prominent musical genres and cultural influences, [and has] . . . four foundational elements . . . [which] include DJing or turntablism, MCing or rapping, B-boying or breaking, and visual graffiti art."[114] Hip-hop continues to bridge the divide between people of different backgrounds. I think back to how I've been able to connect with Black and Brown people on bus or train rides over our mutual taste for hip-hop music and agreement over what the lyrics stand for.

---

113 Rory PQ, "Hip Hop History: From the Streets to the Mainstream," Icon Music Blog, last modified November 25, 2019.

114 Ibid.

This is what I find most meaningful about hip-hop as a musical genre. Collectively, we are aware that hip-hop is bigger than entertainment alone and is one medium for speaking out against inequity.

As I thought about this more, it became easier to identify when people were using hip-hop as a means to feel cool versus a means to share an agenda to fight for a cause. There were distinctions, yet nevertheless, I couldn't bring myself to shake my head at raunchy lyrics because it represented one more win for a community that had dealt with the blow of generational and cultural losses. I found myself a champion of any person of color breaking out on their own and making it. What I've since come to appreciate and personally nod my head to, however, are those hip-hop and rap artists who use their platform to educate or activate their followers to fight against economic, political, and interpersonal inequalities.

Examples of activist-oriented hip-hop around the world include:

- Thousands of organizers in Cape Town, Africa, and Paris, France use hip-hop for activism, addressing environmental justice, policing, prisons, media, and education.
- In Sweden, nongovernmental organizations (NGOs) incorporate graffiti and dance in their engagement of disaffected immigrants and young working-class employees.
- Indigenous communities in Chile, Indonesia, Mongolia, New Zealand, and Norway are using hip-hop to push their views into the local conversation.

- Speakers corner in Hyde Park, one of the royal parks in London, where elements of spoken word, debate, free speech, and hip hop are part of weekly conversations.[115]

While each of these deserves its own documentary, there is one of these I'd like to elaborate on as I experienced it firsthand.

SPEAKER'S CORNER

"What does Black mean to you . . . how should we refer to ourselves? Blacks? Africans?" a tall Black man shouted from a platform in front of a camera, mic, and a steadily growing eager audience of Black and Brown faces huddled together. The brisk September winds swept up leaves in protest as the ringleader pointed his mic in front of others in the circle, daring them to answer. On an unassuming bike ride around Hyde Park in London, I had happened upon this thrilling spectacle. As I looked around, I noticed several dozen circles, much like this one, all engaged in intense discussions. As various members answered, elements of rap and spoken word were mingled in, making the debate lively in more than one way as the vibrations resonated deep within our souls, and our bodies began to unconsciously sync with the cadence of the beat.

Each person was speaking about something important and powerful, but at the same time, those who were still learning their truth could resonate with the familiarity of the beat boxing and in being part of the experience, the community.

---

115 Jeff Chang, "It's a Hip-Hop World."

This is not what I imagined when I first saw the London Eye from the small circular window on the plane, each red, black, and grey building looking as if they fit neatly and perfectly like hair combed back so slick that not a strand is out of place. Leaning against my bike in that park, I felt more comfortable than I had been my whole trip. This exhibition of free thinkers using hip-hop to share their message was something I could resonate with having grown up with it around every corner in America. I can't believe I almost missed this, so I asked around as to what this gathering was—a special occasion or a regular gathering. "Speaker's Corner," an older gentleman nearby said. "It happens every Sunday."

Serendipitously bike riding through Speaker's Corner in Hyde Park, one of the royal parks in London, is one of those rare experiences that one hopes to authentically come across while on a walk or bike ride. The confluence of spoken word, debate, free speech, and hip-hop make these weekly conversations a unique part of Britain's culture.

FOODIE CULTURE

Food also has the power to bring us closer together. Food can communicate culture, hospitality, and fellowship. When spoken languages and customs differ, it is food that can serve as a common ground for connection.

When speaking with people who haven't traveled extensively, I found that food was among the first things they gravitated toward when getting to know a place or learning about a culture. The beauty of this is that with globalization, we can experience cultural and international food close to home without having to travel to another country. Food provides a stepping stone toward cultivating an open mind to the new experiences inherent in a different country by first introducing you to the newness of tastes and textures in what you eat. Food can also provide an excellent opportunity to fuel a country's local economy while experiencing it.

Anthony Bourdain is someone who used his love of food and expertise in the culinary industry to connect with people all over the world. He intentionally explored parts unknown, delved deeper into how food represented a country's history and culture, and broke bread with the locals. His journeys set a roadmap with no start and no ending for how we can adopt a lifestyle of finding quality places to eat that foster cultural experiences.

Anthony left an indelible mark on each person with whom he connected. Upon his passing, many people, including many people of color and members of indigenous communities, came forward with their respect for how he postured his travels and engagements with their culture through food. Anthony represented a "rare traveler they trusted to get their cultures right."[116]

One Trinidadian American states, "I felt I could trust him to see what I saw in Trinidad as if the heart of the country would be safe in his hands as a person and traveler. You trusted him with your heritage."[117]

---

116 Joumana Khatib, "What Anthony Bourdain Meant to People of Color," The New York Times, June 12, 2018.

117 Ibid.

In many ways, Anthony practiced aspects of NVC as he "brought curiosity and empathy to parts of the world that were most unfamiliar to much of his audience. He thought of himself as a guest and was in love with the idea of food as a way to understand the country and its people. He didn't look down on foreign places he visited . . . he saw humanity and food everywhere and connected with it."[118]

There are critiques of Bourdain's approach to visiting African countries for perpetuating "representations of Africa reminiscent of a colonial gaze."[119] These are aspects to be mindful of in how Anthony depicted a country while on his travels, and inherently up for the country's people to decide on how accurately Anthony depicted them and their food.

Nonetheless, even in this inherent difference of opinion on his impact, Bourdain set the stage for a new way of traveling. From the fancy five-course restaurant to the hole in the wall, which specializes in the one cultural dish the locals tell you to try, Bourdain's style was not partial to either. He was a life-long learner of other cultures and sought out authentic connection through appreciating local cuisine. He inspires us to keep an open mind in our own travel experiences through a country's food scene.

---

118 Ibid.

119 Tewodros Workneh and H. Leslie Steeves, "Anthony Bourdain: Parts Unknown in Africa: Cultural Brokerage, "Going Native," and Colonial Nostalgia," International Journal of Communication, 13 (2019).

AN EXCHANGE OF CULTURES THROUGH EDUCATIONAL EXPERIENCES

In learning about third culture kids (TCKs), I became aware of the intentionality of cultural exchanges through study or service, which afford deeply immersive opportunities to experience a place like a local.

In the United States, formal cultural and language exchange programs are those with ties to the Institute of International Education and the Bureau of Educational and Cultural Affairs (ECA) within the US Department of State. These programs are funded to support and encourage mutual understanding between American citizens and citizens of other countries. These exchanges provide opportunities for individuals from different countries to share and appreciate others' perspectives. They can also create a space for cultural understanding as those selected to participate in them serve as bridges between their country and the host country.

International exchange programs are considered a form of cultural diplomacy and advance a greater effort around public diplomacy. International exchanges can include educational, cultural, scholarly, professional, and leadership experiences. While many exchange programs receive funding from the US government, there are several others funded by the nonprofit or for-profit private sector.

I leveraged one such cultural exchange opportunity in the form of the Benjamin A. Gilman Scholarship, funded by the US Department of State, to connect back with my Indian roots. I found that many of my fellow Gilman scholars also used their scholarship to connect to their mother or father's homeland. Several others leveraged the scholarship to expose themselves to an entirely new culture, maintaining an open mind to the customs, food, and language.

My Gilman scholarship afforded me opportunities of which I had only dreamed. Growing up in America automatically removed me from my ethnic upbringing by one degree. I had always yearned to better understand my culture and how other young Indian people grew up, their world views, and customs.

Growing up in a lower-middle class family, our finances were thin to where we did not have opportunities to afford trips or visit the motherland. Nonetheless, I experienced my Hungarian culture through my grandparents, who lived close to us and would introduce us to Hungarian communities and friends in America.

On the other hand, my father was my only family connection to my Indian heritage, as the only person from his immediate family who lived in America. Where we lived in Florida didn't afford too many opportunities to connect with other Indians, and therefore, left me yearning to experience more of my Indian heritage, which is why I ultimately chose India for my study abroad country of choice in college.

Intrigued by the origin of cultural exchange programs, I wondered what elements of my scholarship program could be practiced or applied by the everyday traveler. A few elements that I've repurposed from my Gilman scholarship to other trips abroad include:

- Learning phrases of a language and immersing myself in an environment where I must practice speaking
- Volunteering within the community or for locally driven causes
- Engaging in cultural norms, like practicing yoga while in India
- Making friends
- Experiencing what the locals enjoyed as a pastime

* * *

The concept of culture is not something that necessitates living or visiting another country to experience or understand it. Language, hip-hop, and international food can all be experienced at home. They are also not the only examples of experiencing the culture. They are just among the most prominent in my own travel experiences.

When we realize how much more we have in common, we can create or join that global community.

In reflecting on how you can connect with the world, I encourage you to think about the walls, barriers, and borders we've built up over the centuries.

Perhaps if we took the time to use NVC and understand other cultures, we might not have the same tensions, prejudices, or threats we face today. In reflecting on this, I hope you will see that the world can become a smaller place once we stop seeing and putting up walls and borders between us.

CHAPTER 8

NOMAD AT HEART—A TRIBE WITHOUT BORDERS

———

The wind whipped up mine and the horse's hair as we trotted across the golden pastures with nothing in sight for miles. I wrapped the large green army coat, with wool inside, a little closer to keep warm. The sun would only be out for a couple more hours on this late November day in the Xilamuren Grasslands. My brother, Davin, and I kept up our pace and soon came upon a series of yurts standing out among the vast landscape adorned with the vibrant colors of the Mongolian-Tibetan Buddhist flags. Later that night, we helped gather firewood for the outdoor campfire and tried to keep warm as the temperatures started falling fast. Our tour guide Zorigoo called out that dinner was ready, and as we eagerly greeted the warmth inside the yurt, a robust meal of meat stew, dumplings, and vegetables awaited us. The meat stew, reminiscent of Hungarian Goulash, hit the spot as we chatted with Zorigoo about our Hungarian ancestry and where the connections might exist between our two cultures, considering several of the nomadic tribes from this region traveled and conquered the lands of modern-day Hungary.[120]

As the night started winding down, we went outside to admire the sky, a reminder that we were thousands of miles away from anything familiar.

While the ancestral connection may still be up for debate, our love of the nomadic lifestyle is not. Over the next few days, we embraced sourcing our own campfire fuel from cow dung, using the bathroom outdoors with only the privacy of a rare hill, shooting arrows, and of course, riding horses. This unique experience and the familial connections we felt while there are what solidified that I am a nomad at heart.

MODERN-DAY NOMAD

I'm going to come out and say it: *I hate desks.*

More of an active outdoor person, I like being on the move, whether it's the act of transit itself or while on my travels. As such, I identify as a modern-day nomad, and anytime I have the opportunity to work outside, my stress levels decrease. Living as a nomad also provides an opportunity to live more sustainably because I don't require the space and resources of a normal office environment such as desks and supplies.

---

120 Encyclopedia Britannica Online, s.v. "Inner Mongolia," accessed September 3, 2020.

I do, however, think there are ways to innovate on the concept of a desk to include standing desk risers or platforms to place one's laptop or device on, which can be packed and set up anywhere. You can also take a page out of my book and get comfortable working from your lap with a cooling pad or platform underneath the laptop or device.

My favorite location while working on the road has to be Waikiki Beach in Hawaii. I remember taking a break from my site visit to catch up with my team and my emails. As I ate a poke bowl from the Korean fusion spot down the road and looked out over the horizon of aquamarine waves with my back against the swaying palm tree, I felt like I was living out all those work desktop screen savers or virtual Zoom platform backgrounds. While I wouldn't recommend an extended stay at the beach for remote work, no one could tell the difference as my work wasn't impacted in any way.

While some of you might picture this scene and marvel at how I was even able to get any work done, I would argue that the beach setting provided a sense of calm and rejuvenation, which overshadows the four white walls of an indoor office building. Working outdoors also sparked creativity and enthusiasm to do a good job so that I could justify future opportunities like this one.

Once experimented with remote work one to two days a week, I started thinking about how I could pair this with a trip across the country. I wanted to challenge myself to be adaptable to various settings and scenarios and also flex the muscle of focus and concentration, no matter the setting.

If you have everything you need to do your work, whether that's for an employer or your own business venture, then you can work from anywhere. In most cases, I find that a laptop or tablet, Wi-Fi connection, phone, and the occasional business office perks like sticky notes and mousepads make this possible. However, I understand that not everyone's job will afford them this opportunity. Nonetheless, that doesn't mean it can't or that you can't position yourself for a job that will embrace the work from home lifestyle forever.

Working from home or on the road is the essential ingredient to being a digital nomad.

What is a nomad? According to the encyclopedia, nomads are "individuals who roam about . . . [or] move from place to place."[121]

While some may shake their heads at such a life, I would argue that there are some practices we can learn from nomads who will allow us to be more adaptable to the various things we may encounter in our lives. Therefore, digital nomads "are remote workers who . . . travel to different locations [and] . . . work in coffee shops, co-working spaces, public libraries [and] rely on devices with wireless internet capabilities . . . to do their work wherever they want."[122]

I think many of us could get on board with this alternative American Dream.

---

121 Merriam-Webster, s.v. "nomad (n.)," accessed September 3, 2020.

122 Clifford Chi, "What Is a Digital Nomad and How Do You Become One?" Marketing (blog), HubSpot, March 13, 2020.

There are many ways to prepare for working while traveling or on the road, and that first starts with finding a job where remote working is an option. There are sites like "We Work Remotely and Remote.co, and [one can] ask prospective employers. Freelancing is also a common role for digital nomads."[123]

I believe that in the wake of our global pandemic, many companies, beyond the technology industry, have been working to adapt to a virtual environment and sustain remote work even after the pandemic. Work from home options put the responsibility on the employee and helps foster sustainability by reducing the amount of space, electricity, and other utilities necessary for employers to maintain an in-person workplace.

Through remote work, we can maximize our transit to a particular part of the country or world, which provides opportunities for multi-purpose trips like my work-cation or slower travel experiences, where we can visit with family or friends along with business travel. While we discussed slower travel in the context of finding ourselves in our travels to take the much-needed break from lifestyles that are often unsustainable, the same principles can be applied even when balancing that with productivity.

Slow traveling can extend to exploring sustainable options for business travel, which includes transit by train.

---

123 Ibid.

If this seems counterintuitive to the fast pace of our business sector and how it prioritizes less time for more productivity, that's because it is.

I believe infusing a slower pace in one area can actually sustain a more productive, happier, and healthier workforce, who will feel refreshed each day by their surroundings, while reducing their stress. For example, if I'm on a work trip from Washington, DC to California, I could take the train using their wireless internet to telework while on my way to a conference or meeting instead of catching a flight. I can imagine taking that train ride now. I glance out the window at the treetops or mountainside, beaches, or small towns, and feel the excitement of roaming while doing what I'm most skilled at or what I love.

Why can't we have the option of working from the comfort of a home, plane, or train?

A few skeptics will point out that we might get distracted or slack off.

Not to worry, with the right planning, this too can be avoided.

To manage remote work in a new and unfamiliar location, I found that all I needed was a quiet space, a reliable Internet connection, and a charged phone. If there were little to no meetings, I could take my laptop to work outside. In the past, I've taken a few work calls while on the road, including the mountains of New Hampshire and the Atlantic coastline underneath a lighthouse in Maine. If I'm presenting or leading a call, I'll usually take that from the comfort of my accommodations, wherever that may be. As long as I was prepared for the meeting and had support from other colleagues, I felt comfortable leading or contributing from anywhere.

None of this is possible without flexibility from your company and available resources to include a solid internet connection, working laptop and phone, and back-up options in case the technology doesn't work.

Unfortunately, not everyone will have this option right away because a fair amount of innovation will be needed to think through what aspects of in-person jobs can be streamlined to a virtual environment to give healthcare providers, grocery store workers, delivery workers, technicians, restaurant owners, and other essential workers the option to have a few remote days in between the in-office days. Perhaps there are paperwork or customer service aspects that they can work on remotely, requiring a shift in how businesses do business. Restaurants may need to increase their use of online technologies to provide at-home delivery service. Furthermore, racial disparities exist as less Black and Brown people can work remotely in their current jobs when compared to White people and were also more likely to be laid off or furloughed during the pandemic.[124]

- 16 percent of Hispanic workers can work from home
- 20 percent of Black workers can work from home
- 30 percent of White workers can work from home[125]

---

124 Khiara M Bridges, "How Racial Hierarchy Kills," Time, June 2020, 44.
125 Ibid.

Shifting to remote work would require up-skilling people who don't feel comfortable with technology or whose job has very little interface with these tools. This will be the true test of whether we are equitable in our offerings of remote work options. Once these requirements are met, that's when the real fun can begin with how you responsibly mix in traveling or other pursuits and hobbies. To be responsible will mean setting clear boundaries and expectations for your work, including what hours you will work. Gone are those days of the nine to five; perhaps this more flexible structure will allow us to work when we can do our best work.

In addition to creating an environment where people can work on the road, there are strategies that lead to living a more mobile lifestyle, one where you could pick up and go without the extensive time and burden of planning. This open-mindedness creates more agility versus rigidity. In that openness, you'll find yourself being bolder, taking more risks, and finding peace with going with the flow of moving from place to place with no expectations in mind. Being nomadic in this way can surprise you and lead to some of the most meaningful life-changing experiences. Nomads believe in the sharing community as one that both reduces costs while increasing connections with others.

SHARING ECONOMY

According to Canadian couple Jen and Ted, who have dubbed themselves the thrifty nomads, the sharing economy is "reconnecting modern humanity, providing those without jobs [including] developing countries."[126] The sharing economy can include accommodations platforms such as Airbnb and Couchsurfing, or methods of transportation such as ridesharing and hitchhiking. Sharing resources can result in deeper connections, savings, and reduced carbon footprint. A burgeoning number of companies are already developing platforms and products to make this new kind of travel experience readily available.

While I've never explored Couchsurfing, reading the blogs and guidance from solo female travelers and talking with my friends about their experiences inspired me to maintain an open mind to trying this method of sharing space in the future.

"Couchsurfing is an online platform that connects people from all over the world through hospitality and cultural exchanges . . . [and] saves money on accommodations."[127] According to Budget Travel Babes, Couchsurfing can be a safe option leading to some of your closest friends and proverbial extended family as long as "you know how to use it."[128]

When Couchsurfing, you stay at an accommodation or shelter for free due to an act of generosity or kindness before moving on to the next phase of your journey. Accommodations can vary from luxurious to the bare essentials. There's

---

126 Jen Avery, "The Ultimate List of Sharing Economy Services for Travel," Thrifty Nomads (blog), February 4, 2016.

127 Budget Travel Babes, "Is Couchsurfing safe? How to use Couchsurfing as a solo female traveler," July 1, 2020.

128 Ibid.

no expectation of payment; most of the time it's for company and sharing stories.

Safety tips for Couchsurfing include reading the references of hosts, staying with female hosts, and taking the time to get to know hosts beforehand.

My experiences with Airbnb have followed a similar process, and I've found the filtering tool to be helpful in selecting my preferences. There are also hosts on Airbnb who are rated as superhosts and have achieved this status by consistently gaining positive reviews and bookings on their accommodation.

The openness to Couchsurfing, Airbnb, and hostel culture stems from our openness to meeting new people and forging friendships. Some of those last, while others are but a brief yet wonderful night of human connection and deep conversations. I've forged both short- and long-term relationships with friends across the globe and am always enlightened to learn what impact I've had on them. I've had friends open up their doors or homes to let me know there's a bed, a room, or a meal for me when I'm in town and have made good on that offer during domestic travels around America.

STRANGERS TO FRIENDS
My African American friend DaQuawn, who won a study abroad scholarship and decided to explore Senegal in Africa, has mastered the art of sharing on his travels by establishing meaningful friendships.

"Sometimes you have to be open to being the fool in the room, being vulnerable, but it's something that can instill a bond in them later," he stated as he recounted the story behind his international friendships.

Every time I talk to him, he has a new story about how he just spoke to his friend in Morocco, or how he's planning his next excursion to Spain to do some human centered design workshop, or he's visiting Senegal for yet another year. It is that ease with which he speaks of these connections as friends that has me revisiting some of my own international connections to see if there really is the foundation of a friendship there.

DaQuawn mentioned how key his travel experiences and ability to sustain and budget travel was dependent on making friends and Couchsurfing. Making friends has always been easier in the environment of locals or local-led tour companies, which is why I appreciate hostel culture and what it has to offer. I met a group of fellow hostellers a couple of years back in Scotland, and it enriched the experience tenfold. The types of places we stay in also have a huge impact.

On a free walking tour, we visited a foundation and cafe that worked on rehabilitating the lives of those who were impoverished, in recovery, or homeless. The tour guide told us the beautiful history of how the foundation was now staffed and run by the initial clients of the organization who had come to the facility for a bed, a meal, and a new purpose. Both the foundation and my tour guide continue to pay it forward by promoting the organization's work to tourists which keep those who were once homeless, in meaningful careers.

When you make friends on your travels or meet with people who are from various other places, the world becomes a little smaller. The ability to mobilize and travel soon becomes more attainable, more comfortable, and more affordable, especially if it's a friend with whom you're staying. At the same time, it can't just be one-sided where every time you need that crash-pad in Hackney, you reach out on WhatsApp messenger, a global text messaging service, to your friends in the United Kingdom (UK) for an assist—true story. When you can make true and lasting friendships, it goes without saying.

As for the story, I stayed at a friend's place near Hackney when my Airbnb fell through in London one late pre-winter evening. We had maintained a mostly virtual friendship up to that point, introduced through their cousin with whom I had gone to college. Before arriving in London, I had mentioned I would be passing through for a day or two on my way to Germany. So, as I was walking through the craggy winding streets of downtown London looking for the Airbnb and only meeting storefronts, I quickly thumbed through my contacts to just reach out and mention I had arrived and would be open to meeting up that evening. I wanted to experience what London nightlife was like, and my friend was already out but emphasized we remain in touch until I was ready and then would meet up. The next two hours were made up of frustration after frustration as I was unable to find the apartment I had booked through Airbnb, unable to get in touch with the host. Then my phone died, and of course, the outlets are different, and I didn't have a universal charger on my person at the time.

I have since learned to always travel with one carry-on.

In a bind, I was trying to figure out how I would charge my phone. I wove in and out of Turkish and Indian restaurants in the neighborhood, asking for a charger as mine wouldn't work with the outlets. I finally got lucky with one Turkish restaurant owner who was able to charge my phone with his charger, and by the time I got enough juice, it was already close to midnight. I tried to find the Airbnb apartment again and still no such luck. I thought I found what might have been the apartment on the second floor of a storefront, but it was boarded up, and there were no visible entryways. I certainly couldn't climb, jump, or fly my way up to the windowsill to check it out.

I assessed my options at that point and decided a seven-hour trek through London and its nightlife might not be so bad, even though I had my backpack—yes, I recommend always traveling with one for these reasons—with me. I could check that into coat check if I ended up at a bar or lounge. I knew to get around quickly, especially to the areas of London that would be open on a night like this, I would need to take public transit via their Tube, closer to center city.

Imagine my dismay when I had finally resolved to sticking it out for the next few hours in London only to find that the Tube closest to me was closing and not accepting additional riders for the night.

At this point, I knew things might only get more difficult, so I reached out to my friend to see what ideas they had, which eventually led to a cab ride at 2 a.m. to Hackney with me assessing my accommodation choices. I've since then had much more pleasant experiences with Airbnb, so this should by no means discourage you from testing out the service and platform yourself since some of them have been among the best in accommodations, but in starting out, I am blessed I had an option at that moment through a chance friendship I had cultivated while in college.

* * *

Securing a safe and relatively enjoyable trip ensures an opportunity for others. Planning what to pack, what to see, and how much time you'll have during your entire trip is essential, too. This can also be done with those you are traveling with over a series of phone calls, meet-ups, or video chats. These provide opportunities to build up excitement for the upcoming journey and also make space for everyone's collective knowledge about what might be needed for the trip, which often highlights gaps in one's own thinking about what to prepare for. Planning also includes preparing for if and when things don't go according to plan. That way, you are at least ready for the mistakes, missed engagements, and the unexpected.

We'll revisit planning for the unplanned and leverage the lessons learned from scary situations as we delve into the next mindset of resilience and how it can help us overcome fears related to traveling.

PART IV

RESILIENCE

Unlike most people whose instincts tell them to run when frightened, this woman's inner voice urged her to challenge and confront her fears head-on.

—RICK SMOLAN ABOUT ROBYN DAVIDSON,
2,700-KILOMETER SOLO FEMALE TREKKER
WHO TRAVELED ON FOOT ACROSS
THE AUSTRALIAN OUTBACK

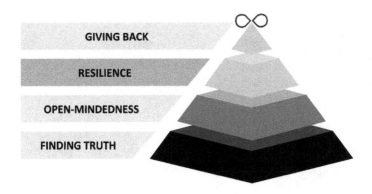

Resilience is the growth mindset we adopt on the road as we take risks, overcome our fears, and develop confidence in our abilities to circumnavigate the world. Apply lessons learned from past experiences. Adapt to the unexpected. Where roadblocks exist, remain open to taking paths that lead to new possibilities.

CHAPTER 9

THE FOUR SEASONS OF OVERCOMING FEAR—A ROCKY ROAD TO RESILIENCE

———

ALONE IN THE DARK SOLO TRAVELING

I remember that first night camping alone in Patagonia. I could see pumas running in the distant foothills chasing the wintry-spring air, which whispered through naked tree branches amid a dramatic sky of more stars than I've ever seen. The mountains of Torres del Paine National Park were looming in the distance, forewarning me of the twenty-kilometer hike I would soon take to the Mirador Base Las Torres. My worries were increasing as fast as the light was fading, and I knew I needed to pitch my tent soon. Accomplishing the first feat of my camper's rite of passage in less than thirty minutes, I had nothing but time ahead of me. I planned to get up before sunrise and bundled up to keep warm amid temperatures still reminiscent of winter. After spending a couple of hours fighting for the last bit of warmth from my sleeping bag, I started to hear scratching noises against the tent. I thought it was a puma, snake, or some other wild animal and just stayed still as I tried to fall back asleep.

Eventually, I became fed up with the ambiguity of the noise and shouted at the dark while unzipping my tent. As I looked around, waving the flashlight wildly in the dark with a hiking stick in my hand, I heard the same noise behind me. Ready to fight whatever was keeping me awake, I realized it was only the wind and cracked tree branches fueling an imagination of fears.

I took a breath, laughed at myself and my pretty little fears, realizing the reality was much more mundane as I went back to sleep.

Similarly, in traveling with others and speaking to friends about their own trips, I began to notice how others' big or little fears impacted how much they would be willing to experience.

Personally, what helped me overcome fear is my love of the horror genre. While tackling fears by watching and reading things that make one scared seems counterintuitive, the approach helped me understand what fear is and why it exists. There are several components of good horror films or books that show us how to overcome fear. The genre has also personally influenced me to not let things get to me as much and to have a plan for when they start to invade my mind or imagination. Because horror can unearth those things that scare us most, overcoming fear at its core is simply under-standing what makes us afraid.

Additionally, in learning about my escapism patterns in the finding truth mindset, I could better prepare myself for tackling them in the resilience mindset. For that reason, if you don't know what you are running from or what you are afraid of, I encourage you to spend some additional time finding the truth before you dive into practicing the aspects of resilience outlined here.

I took time to understand my fears and have backup plans prepared, but ultimately, I knew that my trip could veer off course, and ultimately, it would be up to me to be ready to embrace that as part of the journey. As one of my initial experiences in solo traveling, Chile helped me grow into a stronger traveler and a stronger person.

MITIGATING RISKS

"Travel is inherently risky," my African American friend Ter-rell said, as we were catching up on a video call and talking about his recent trip to Patagonia.

"There's no such thing as safe [because] anytime you go to a different place, anything could happen."

He recounted a few stories about how he and his wife took a bike ride in the rural countryside of China. Before they knew it, they were lost without a Wi-Fi signal, and then their bikes broke. While in the moment, both of them focused on how to safely navigate out of that situation, Terrell fondly reminisces,

"This is why travel is fun. Those things can happen [and it's] about practicing managing risk. When I was out there in Patagonia, I had to figure out [the learning curve] knowing it gets better . . . as long as you can handle the initial dip."

What Terrell was saying holds true to experiencing and adapting to any new place. There will be a period of time where you may be the fool, make mistakes, get lost, or end up in a less than ideal situation. What matters is how you make it past that initial setback without letting it interrupt or ruin the experience of being somewhere else. That's not to say preparation can't help avoiding these pitfalls, for as Terrell notes, "We were climbing mountains [and] my class-mates nearly broke their legs. That would have changed the trip for sure [because we were] in a remote wilderness." In this situation, Terrell and his classmates were pushing them-selves to their limits, which could have resulted in injury. Luckily, they paced their hikes and were honest with where they were on the learning and hiking curve. Whether you are pushing yourself or putting yourself in a situation that will require hyper-awareness of your surroundings, having a plan in place can be incredibly valuable.

It's this level of planning that my friend Carole infused in her solo travels throughout Central and South America that gave her the confidence to get back out on the road after having experienced a scare on one of her trips.

OVERCOMING DANGER & TRAUMA

Carole experienced a different kind of fear based on a traumatic experience during her solo travels in Central and South America.

She breathed in the fresh mountain air on her walk around the church grounds in Colombia. She felt a sense of awe and humility as she realized she was playing a role she recently came to know all too well, that of a trusted presence. These Colombian women had seen and lived through much tragedy. Some of them were addicted to drugs, while others wrapped up in the vicious cycles of violence, drugs, and sex work. She strongly believed in the mission of the family she was staying with, who were also religious leaders at the congregation. They started this charity a few months before to provide opportunities for women with these experiences and gave them a place to stay.

"When I first started traveling, I was more or less comfortable with finding my way around and with the thrill of being in a new place [figuring things] out," Carole reminisced about her year of traveling through Central and South America.

Also, a solo female traveler, Carole was aware of the inherent risks. However, allured by the newness of experiences in other countries, she remained open and "maybe a little naïve" as she connected with people whose personalities she seemed to click.

Then things got real.

The music, the food, the people, Carole loved it all as she found herself making friends while on a solo trip across Central America. On one of her trips, she followed someone whom she believed was going to show her more of the local culture. As they continued walking, she soon found herself in a predicament she could not easily get out of and realized she was being abducted. Carole was held in a building for an unknown amount of time before she was finally able to escape and return home safely, but the experience haunted her.

I could hear the bravery and unwavering power behind her voice as she recounted being abducted during one of her trips. As she relived that moment and what she had to do to put herself back out on the road, she confidently said, "There's just so much beauty and joy in experiencing these different things . . . I love traveling by myself and putting myself in these scenarios where I'm staying in a more open group setting and can meet different people. I don't think that [an experience] should necessarily change that in the way you travel." I was inspired and admired her mental courage in how she maintained a sense of calm under what I could only imagine had to be a very traumatic experience to get through. Naturally and respectfully, I wanted to know more, especially as someone who solo travels quite often.

After navigating out of that scary situation, Carole returned home to the US and took the time she needed to recover. She was very tactful about what she did next, knowing the importance of feeling, processing, and eventually, healing was key to any future travels.

Carole's ability to recover and heal from her trauma is represented in Medellin, Colombia, the first city Carole visited when she embarked on her solo travels once more.

MAKE LOVE NOT WAR

My friends and I were on a free walking tour in Colombia, following our vibrant and warm tour guide around Community Thirteen or Comuna Trece in Medellin, which at one point, used to be the most dangerous place to go in Colombia. "Today is Sunday, which means you'll see a lot of people dancing and relaxing in the barrio," our tour guide said as he hummed a tune on his lips and swayed his hips to the sounds of the Afro-Latina reggaeton echoing up and down the mural-filled streets.

We were in awe as he explained the significance behind the art on the walls and buildings throughout the community. A deeper meaning than simply graffiti, the artists were telling the story of their lives, of the struggles they had overcome from the days of guerillas and drugs, and the hope that was revived as the community started to shed its dangerous past and turn into a place filled with music, art, and a love for one another.

Comuna Trece is a good example of an entire community overcoming the dangers of violence and navigating the trauma associated with its past. The community has emerged more resilient today as it claims one of the top destinations in

Colombia and South America.[129] Comuna Trece experienced a significant transformation, in large part due to the community pulling together to make a home out of the tragedies that befell them for years. Once the community banded together, tourism started increasing, and the effect was positive once as it continued to transform the community for the better.[130]

From 1996 to 2002, Comuna Trece was the most dangerous place in Colombia and "third most violent district on the planet [due to] turf wars between guerrilla forces, paramilitaries, and the government resulting in some of the bloodiest [and deadliest] battles of this civil war," according to the nonprofit e-news outlet, Colombia Reports.[131]

In 2008, the city's government started expanding public transportation options that connected Comuna Trece to the rest of Medellin, including a cable car network, subway, and series of escalators that allowed residents to access the highest parts of the district, normally 480 meters of steps.[132] Many of the locals stepped up to run their own programs, organize cultural and sports activities, and open up businesses (i.e., tours, coffee shops, book shops, galleries) the moment they saw foreigners appearing on the outskirts of their town.

As a means to remember their past and paint a picture of their future, artists started creating colorful murals all over

---

129 Adam Veitch, "Comuna 13: How a Medellin community turned a war zone into a tourist attraction," Colombia Reports, June 14, 2019.

130 Ibid.

131 Ibid.

132 Ibid.

the community. As tourism increased, the people viewed foreigners visiting as a source of cultural pride for how much they've overcome. The accessibility of Comuna Trece continues to play a huge role in sustaining its positive transformation with the increase in both mass public transit and flights from other countries to Medellin.[133]

THE FOG OF FOUR SEASONS

One of the moments I felt the most fear was when I didn't know what was next for my life, professionally or personally. It felt like a fog. These moments would happen every few weeks like a perpetual cycle of confusion with no clear destination.

The jarring shifts in Haunting of Bly Manor reminded me of my own life in uncanny ways.[134] So much about that season resonated, and it was the only thing that seemed to make sense to me as I sought out advice, sought to find myself again after months of trauma and burnout.

What is wrong with me? I thought. Every effort was futile toward the goal of getting back to my normal or some semblance of it. Like the characters of Bly Manor, I felt like I was in a daze when facing loss or guilt, not wishing to relive the moments I had escaped. Sometimes I was in denial over what trauma had occurred. All I knew was I was not okay, and it had been this way for too long of a time.

---

133 Ibid.

134 Haunting of Bly Manor, directed by Mike Flanagan, written by Mike Flanagan, aired October 9, 2020, on Netflix.

"Why does this keep happening to me?" Flora screamed at the air with exasperation as she continued, "I don't like this game."[135]

There are times when the plans we have for life go awry in the most disastrous or perhaps spectacular of ways. When I'm in the fog, I can't see the spectacular.

The characters would go through what was called "dream-hopping," a trick their mind would play to avoid having to face something even more traumatic or scary, but in doing so, these moments where they would slip would bring them face to face with a pivotal memory that had started the slipping or hopping, to begin with.[136] I knew I had started feeling this on my travels when the sheer amount became too much to handle.

I wanted to play the hero, put on my big-girl pants, and tell myself I could handle these feelings of burnout and sadness that I've been through worse. It's during these moments in which I practice mindfulness, which I picked up in the finding truth mindset, and reflect with gratitude on that trip to Patagonia.

In some ways, when I embarked on my hike in Patagonia, I didn't know what to expect. I had overcome a slight fear in the night camping and sleeping alone out in the wild, and that felt like a win, but now I faced the true test of strength in front of me, and what was worse, I couldn't see anything

---

135 Ibid.

136 Ibid.

with the fog blanketing the path at 5 a.m. that morning. I had hiked before, but nothing close to the length of this trail, and knowing how long a trail is doesn't exactly feel the same as when you are on that path, and minute after minute feels like hours. The fog started to clear with a light spring misting of the air as I pulled my waterproof coat closer around me. The first couple hours of my hike soon beckoned like the spring.

I paused to take a breath and pulled out my snacks when the fog returned, the clouds greyed, and out of nowhere, it started snowing. I found refuge under a thicket of branches but looked incredulously at the sky. I knew to expect this, but it seemed sudden after the first few hours of spring weather.

As soon as it cleared, a group had caught up to me, and we carried on for a while together, shedding coats and jackets as the temperature started to rise with the incline. I checked with someone on the temperature, and we were nearing the seventies, which seemed impossible given the snowstorm I just witnessed during my lunch. But here we were, sweating from the hike and the warmth, in summer.

As we neared the most difficult part of the hike, we were met once more with snow, this time several feet deep on the trail ahead, covering treacherous rocks and iced rivers and streams. I had my hiking sticks, which added resistance and grip along the rocky terrain.

Reaching the peak and Mirador de Las Torres at the top was a dreamscape of another land, another time. And then it was over almost as soon as it had arrived, for I knew the journey back would be long, and I didn't want to think about hiking in the pitch-black dark. On the decline, there was a moment where I passed through a patchwork of trees with golden and burnt orange leaves that fell from branches, littering the ground beneath it. The temperature was falling to a cool fifty degrees, and the ambience gave off an air of fall. I made it back to my camp by twilight, too exhausted to pitch a tent for a moment, as I passed out near the shelter with an immense sense of satisfaction.

I had experienced all four seasons on this hike, a phenomenon that would normally happen in the context of a year. I thought about how this could be a metaphor for life, not just literally with our seasons, but in how quickly the time would pass before we were surprised with the greeting of a new one. I thought about how the only way to make it through the flurry of seasons on this rocky road was through the resilience that comes from continuing forward.

This movement forward is something that served me well on another trip through the winding streets of Hong Kong on the night I got lost.

EMBRACING DETOURS

I've had my fair share of experiences not going according to plan. I fondly reminisce and laugh about them now, but in the moment, these experiences were stressful and left me feeling out of control, which can be scary.

Maybe they could have been avoided, but there will always be something else that occurs in its place that might deviate from our carefully curated plans, and what I've learned is that how you respond matters over anything else.

I was taking in the misty and cool night while navigating through Hong Kong's hilly streets, looking for a bus that would never arrive to go across the bridge to the other side of the city where I was staying. According to the Internet, the bus should have been here by now, but it had almost been an hour and the time ticked on. Thus began hour one of what ended up being a five-hour journey through the city, including standing at bus stations that echoed a deafening silence to pleading with a cab driver to have the decency to at least take us across the bridge because walking across was illegal and punishable by a fine and jail time. The driver did the bare minimum, but at least we were closer, and the view as we got out of the car and walked across the shipping ports was a high wave of lights amid pitch black buildings and mountains. Then began the guessing game of which street or series of streets seemed closest to the Airbnb, which was on a main strip of the city near the planetarium.

As my phone had already died, the journey itself was a testament to the perseverance that only comes with persistence and an exercise in long-term memory and navigation skills. After two hours, the streets began to look familiar, and relief washed over me like a wave upon seeing the building where at last, a bed and hot shower awaited. The experience was a lesson in having back-up chargers for phones, being prepared for the uncertainty of transit (public and private alike), and not giving up. It's easy to have reacted with a defeated squat on the sidewalk in frustration while cursing and crying at the empty roads, but a willing attitude eventually conquered amid the odds stacked high like Hong Kong's cityscape. While exhausting, I found gratitude in the experience afterward because at least the view was nice. I imagine that once I have the chance to return, I'll greet its streets like a familiar neighborhood dog or cat.

The Hong Kong experience also shaped my future travel behavior in that it made me feel more comfortable with exploring my immediate surroundings and walking the unfamiliar streets in whatever neighborhood I might be staying in. It also encouraged me to challenge myself in finding my way back to my accommodations without the aid of maps or technology. This is a strategy my friend DaQuawn embraced to feel more comfortable with unfamiliar surroundings.

* * *

The anxious anticipation DaQuawn felt as he stepped off the public transit subway in the middle of a foreign country, not knowing where he had gotten off, was both frightening and exciting. The moment called upon his inner explorer and ability to adapt. By first being open-minded, he was able to create opportunities for new experiences he wouldn't have normally considered on his trip. His resilient mindset then showed itself in how he embraced the thrill and challenge of finding his way through the streets of a country unknown to him. When finding his way proved unsuccessful, it forced him out of his comfort zone as he engaged with the locals to ask for directions. What DaQuawn soon found was that if he engaged in genuine, deep conversations, they would lead to lifelong friendships. In some instances, DaQuawn was invited to have dinner or stay with some of the friends he made abroad after getting to know each other better. This level of trust in oneself and the larger global community is not only admirable but something from which we can all learn.

HITCHHIKING FOR THE JOURNEY, NOT THE DESTINATION

I may have a destination in mind or a certain outcome I'm hoping for with my travels and even my life. I'm focused on the destination. It's not so much about the destination; it's about the journey. This same principle applies to hitchhiking.

Hitchhiking opens up adventures between origin and destination, point A to point B.

Full disclaimer, I have never tried this myself, but I've been inspired to do so even more after hearing about world traveler Tomislav's experience and talking with my brother about his own hitchhiking endeavors through Iceland.

"I hitchhiked, I traveled in cars, trucks, motorcycles, on horses, boats, buses, trains, and rickshaws. I worked many odd jobs, spent time with locals, volunteered, [got my head shaved by a monk], and sailed across the Indian Ocean. And I did all of that with almost no money."[137]

---

137 Tomislav Perko, "How to travel the world with almost no money," filmed February 2015 at TEDxTUHH, Hamburg University of Technology, Hamburg, Germany, video.

Back when the stock market crashed in 2008, due to the failure of several large US companies, and the housing bubble burst, Tomislav was among the many thousands who lost their jobs, money, and purpose.

During that time, Tomislav felt lost and that his life lacked meaning, but he was determined to recover this and started doing his research on traveling the world as a way to reignite that spark. He generally knew that traveling expenses would fall into three major categories, transportation cost, accommodations, and everything else (i.e., food, entertainment, tours). Tomislav was initially afraid of leaving his comfort zone and his home of Croatia, to be alone in the unknown world with no money. "You don't have to be brave or rich when you travel," he said. "I sure wasn't [when I started]."[138]

Right before leaving Croatia on his round the world trip, people told him to exercise caution with hitchhiking and couch surfing and that when he crossed the border into Serbia, he might get killed.[139] He had an amazing experience in Serbia, stayed with people, developed friendships and upon hitching a ride to the Bulgarian border, heard a similar tale from the driver about being mindful of the gypsies there and that he might get killed. And yet, the experience was more of the same, truly hospitable people, amazing experiences. "It wasn't just a travel lesson. It was a life lesson not to trust all the horror stories people tell," Tomislav said with the confidence of someone who had learned to take a leap of faith in

---

138 Ibid.

139 Ibid.

humanity.[140] Tomislav took the leap of faith to get out of his comfort zone and embrace the growth of learning through experience. He soon found that it could often be cheaper to travel in this way than to live in his own city.

While hitchhiking can certainly bring about thoughts of horror movies based on the true stories which depicted an increase in America's serial killers in the eighties, Tomislav braved the nightmares and practiced hitchhiking on most of his trips.

Now you might catch yourself stopping and saying, "Hitch-hiking is not for me, period."

I will encourage you to adopt the open-minded mindset for a moment and continue thinking about how hitchhiking is much more about an exercise in developing relationships with complete strangers than it is about putting yourself in danger on the road. At times, I caught myself laughing and feeling heart-warmed by the stories and videos Tomislav shared on his hitchhiking adventures.

"Was it worth it? Definitely, yes," he emphasized as he ticked through the personal truths he had found and learned that the world is not as scary of a place as the media or others make it out to be.[141] While hitchhiking, Tomislav grew out of his prejudices, learning that "people around the world are

---

140 Ibid.

141 Ibid.

the same, no matter how we try to point to all the differences in race, culture, and religion."[142]

I also decided to speak to my brother, Davin, who had first-hand experience with hitchhiking and had delved into getting and giving rides while making lifelong friends along the way. Something you have to understand about Davin is that he grew up as a Boy Scout in swampy central Florida and eventually made his way to the frosted forests of Michigan for high school and college. Between the survivalist life hacks learned from Scouts and the extreme temperature changes in his teens, he's adapted to his fair share of surprises. With that under his belt, he boldly tried his hand at hitchhiking on his first solo trip.

In August 2017, he was in Iceland, the start of his solo hiking and backpacking trip. The people he was traveling with were going to continue their journey. After their hike to the top of Vatnajokull, he planned to hitchhike back to Reykjavik. He gave himself a decent buffer and had accommodations booked at a hostel. It was just a matter of when he would show up. Part of what he didn't plan for was the frequency of cars from where he started (he was on a side road versus the main Ring Road). It was thirty minutes before he got a car to stop. Two Hollanders were going to the next town over, and he rode for twenty minutes with them even though they were not going exactly where he needed to go. It was another hour and a half before he got picked up again. When doing this, you won't know when you'll get a ride, it could be one right after another, or there can be a couple of hours between rides.

---

142 Ibid.

During this second ride, the guy took him to the closest town over from where he was staying. It was getting later and later, and he needed to plan accurately since he wanted to be in Reykjavik by the evening. At that point, he had to decide between hitchhiking (while being unsure of the time that'd take), or he could take a bus directly there. He decided to play it safe and take the bus. He could have kept going in this way but figured it was his best option due to the time. It really comes down to your comfort level. "It's such a great way to connect with people and get around on a budget, but more importantly, it's about those connections you make along the way," he said.

Davin suggests that the approach can't be, "I need to get from point A to point B in this time frame because in most cases, it won't line up. Halfway through, I realized I didn't have time."

That's the second variable, time.

"When you have a more laissez-faire approach to travel, Couchsurfing and hitchhiking can work well."

I agreed.

Because of factors outside of your control, it would be difficult to have a regimented itinerary for hitchhiking. Davin emphasizes it's important to be open to how you travel and where you stay as you constantly adapt your time expectations.

"It might take three days versus one day if you were to go directly to the destination."

Thinking about Tomislav's rules, Davin's experiences, and referencing several bloggers' tips for catching rides with strangers, I curated rules of the hitchhiking road for you to consider. These rules can be used beyond the context of catching a ride. They can be applied when talking to strangers, going to a new place, getting lost, embracing a detour, or overcoming fear on that rocky road.

RULES OF THE HITCHHIKING ROAD

1. Stay positive, be in a good mood, be happy.
2. Pick a good spot to get picked up and be on the right side of the road heading in the right direction. Cars need to be able to stop safely.
3. Get out of cities and toward main highways or roads.
4. Use the universal signs, which include either a thumbs up or a cardboard sign with big clear writing on where your destination is and a funny or personable message.
5. Look presentable and decent, wear clean clothes (and maybe a travel-related shirt, so people know you are there to travel).
6. Look relatable, as people tend to feel comfortable picking up people who look like them or look like they have similar tastes (e.g., shirt with hip-hop quote or sports-related gear).
7. Avoid nighttime.
8. Be confident by smiling and making good eye contact with the driver.
9. Hitchhike with a friend.
10. Make conversation with your drivers, because that's the only way you can repay them (often they are interested to hear your travel stories); if not, you can listen to theirs.

11. Fasten your seatbelt if you have one.
12. Practice good passenger etiquette (e.g., when a driver is tired or asleep, offer to drive).
13. Be patient and prepared with food, water, and snacks to share; you might wait a while.
14. Challenge yourself to get out of your comfort zone to see the world and people.
15. Use common sense and trust your instincts when choosing a ride. You are not obligated to accept the ride if something does not feel right.
16. Stay in control by maintaining your confidence, keeping your valuables close, and calling a friend with your whereabouts or by posting them on social media.
17. Avoid arguments and controversial topics.[143]

In all these experiences, the individual or individuals are continually assessing and mitigating risk. Perhaps they face their own insecurities or in other situations dealing directly with unknowns that disrupt their plans and place them in dangerous situations. To leave our comforts and homes in place of something unfamiliar already requires us to exercise bravery, which ultimately leads to feeling more prepared to handle any situation that comes your way.

Additionally, if we are overcoming trauma, the healing process is not a simple formula or a quick fix.

---

143 "How to travel the world with almost no money," Tomislav Perko, accessed May 6, 2020; "14 Ways to Safely Hitchhike Across the United States," Nomadic Matt, accessed May 6, 2020.

Finding truth and open-minded mindsets are aspects of self-realization that is important to your growth as an individual. The resilience mindset is where you begin to apply the new ways you've developed as a person, for the better. The longer you spend in a mindset or revisit it, the stronger you are in that particular area and the easier it will be to exhibit that on your travels.

We don't always know what our destination will consist of when we visit another place. Anything could go wrong. We could hop on the wrong train, we could miss our flight, or we could stay within the confines of an orderly preordained itinerary that may or may not work for us. I'm careful not to be too prescriptive with my travels now as someone who spent the first two years detailing itineraries and conducting research about each place. Still, be prepared. The preparation is what helps you, it's your resource as you may go through the journey that can fuel you along the way, but if it's too rigid, it might leave you unsatisfied, stressed, or worse, not living in that moment that is being in another environment completely unfamiliar to you and trying it on for fit as a lifestyle.

Once you target your fear, you can prepare for it with reflection through mental exercises that outline possible scenarios to make you more proactive for when you do face a similar situation. As such, I've prepared an exercise for you as the traveler to keep in mind the next time you feel particularly vulnerable or afraid on a trip.

Overcoming Fear & Danger Exercise

Action: Isolate the source of fear and name it.

Questions	Your answer
Who's the villain, monster, or bad person?	
What's the scary thing?	

Horror Genre Examples

Naming your monster can be therapeutic because it puts a face, a title to the thing that most elicits such a strong sense of helplessness. It's no longer this completely unfathomable thing that you can't understand. And some scary things are the result of natural things out of our control and what makes them scary to us is our inability to do something about it, so your source in this instance is your lack of control.

Action: Understand the motivation behind the source of fear.

Questions	Your answer
What makes this person or object scary?	
What does the scary person or object want? And how does that affect you?	

Horror Genre Examples

Some scary things or people are getting their version of vengeance or are miserable and want others to feel their pain or hurt.

Some objects or situations are scary to us because they are foreign and represent the unknown. If we can't control for them, we have no idea what the outcome will be as we embark on that path.

Action: Use common sense and non-violent communication principles.

Questions	Your answer
Where do you have the upper hand?	
Is there anything in your environment that you can use or keep close at hand to make you feel safe?	

Horror Genre Examples

Don't let curiosity become your downfall. In the movies, the first to hear a noise and go check it out is the first to check out of the movie. If you hear something, don't look.

If you find yourself in a situation where a stranger wants to take you to a shady, abandoned place, don't follow. Open-mindedness ends where common sense begins. Use non-violent communication principles to determine others' motives.

If it's too late for that, look around your environment and follow the next action step.

Action: Have an exit strategy.

Questions	Your answer
What's your escape plan?	
What does a favorable outcome look like?	

Horror Genre Examples

Most Horror movies build-up to a release. In the end, the protagonist escapes or defeats the monster.

Think about how you would get out of this situation if it were to become threatening.

Walk through different scenarios and play them out like alternate cut-scenes to see if you fare better. If not, dial back your actions before you're too committed.

Action: Get out with your life, your limbs, and a lesson.

Questions	Your answer
Have you awakened from the nightmare?	
What have you learned in the process?	

Horror Genre Examples

Like most protagonists who narrowly escape their monsters, you may be tempted to look back. Don't. Prioritize getting to safety.

Remember the how and why the events transpired. Learn from the experience.

CHAPTER 10

CRISIS AND POST-CRISIS TRAVELING

THE RISKS OF TRAVELING DURING CRISIS

The bulldozer drove through the lush tropical forests in inland Hong Kong, China. It knocked down the palm tree a family of bats lived in, and they had to move. They fed on a diseased mammal from their stoop, a piece of it falling in a pigsty. One pig ate it, and then the local farmer sold it to the local chef, who used his bare hands to prepare it for cooking. An American woman wanted to meet the chef, and they shook hands, posed for a picture, and two weeks later, a global pandemic unfolds.[144]

While subtle, the ending scene of this movie was a reminder of how deforestation can ultimately lead to a pandemic like the one depicted in Contagion.[145] Even more sobering to

---

144 Contagion, directed by Steven Soderbergh (Los Angeles, CA: Warner Bros. Studio, 2011), on Amazon Prime.

145 Ibid.

think about is whether we would be prepared to handle a natural global disaster of that scale.

Ultimately, it is up to the audience to determine what to blame for the global crisis, but Contagion presents several options, including environmental, travel, careless hygiene practices, and misinformation, which can spread even more rapidly than the others as the urge to feed into our darkest fears manifest when we don't know enough information. The first patient's actions depict her unknowingly spreading the infection to countless other tourists and international business travelers in the restaurant. This scene which depicts a super-spreader incident.[146]

* * *

The Scientific American covered super-spreader incidents detailing that they happen when "one person infects a disproportionate number of other individuals," and they "[play] an oversized role in the transmission of [a] virus."[147]

As such, super-spreader events for COVID-19 and the people involved or responsible for them have spurred massive criticism online.

With our increasing participation on the internet comes an increase in the cacophony of noise as everyone attempts to have their voice heard, and the masses are persuaded by who

146 Ibid.

147 Christie Aschwanden, "How 'Superspreading' Events Drive Most COVID-19 Spread," Scientific American, June 23, 2020.

makes the better argument or perhaps has the most dramatic delivery, whether or not what they are promoting is based on scientific fact. And while misinformation continues to spread about the virus, the New Yorker details that what's equally destructive is online public shaming as people "around the world . . . who spread the coronavirus . . . face both a dangerous illness and an onslaught of online condemnation."[148]

From the end of February to mid-March, Nga Nguyen, who is a travel and couture influencer on Instagram, flew from her home-base in London to Milan to France to London to Germany.[149] Nga's sister Nhung joined her in Milan, France, and London before flying back home to Hanoi, Vietnam.

You're probably thinking, that's a lot of flying. Did they catch COVID-19?

Yes. Both sisters and tested positive for the virus. As one of them was an influencer, they were both publicly shamed on the internet once news spread online.

"The Vietnamese government [was] committed to making an example of Nhung [and disclosed] that when she flew home from London, she did not mention her visit to Italy."[150] Furthermore, officials noted she had infected her sister and was the "probable source of infection" for ten people on her flight

---

148 D.T. Max, "The Public-Shaming Pandemic," The New Yorker, Annals of Psychology, September 21, 2020.

149 Ibid.

150 Ibid.

who tested positive, her driver, housekeeper, and an aunt.[151] Vietnam wasn't the only country to crackdown. After seven of the airplane passengers who tested positive were identified as British, the Daily Mail critiqued the sisters, specifically calling out Nhung as a "globe-trotting super-spreader who attended fashion shows around Europe."[152]

In this instance, I know several will relate and cry out in indignation about how someone could fly to all these different countries during the peak of global spread. And many thousands on the Internet did cry out and shame the sisters as decadent and careless.

Others will sympathize with and forgive the ignorance or lack of awareness that comes with not understanding prevention measures and the full context behind how COVID-19 spread.

WHEN ONE ISSUE ECLIPSES ANOTHER

Another pandemic I alluded to in this journey toward promoting sustainable travel is that of racism. The egregiousness of the murders of Black people across America was enough to eclipse COVID-19 for a moment as people came out to protest and march despite the recommendations for social distancing. While age-old, each generation must come face

---

151 Ibid.

152 Connor Boyd, "Globe-trotting Vietnamese daughter of a steel magnate 'infected SEVEN Britons who shared a plane with her with coronavirus' after attending Gucci and Saint Laurent fashion shows in Milan and Paris," Daily Mail, March 11, 2020.

to face with its own call to action for civil rights. Perhaps all the idealism in our youth stemming from the audacious courage exhibited by those who conducted and participated in the March for Our Lives two years before made for the right ingredients, but I saw such a passion for doing something to call to attention that racism was also unnecessarily taking lives, and disproportionately, Black lives.

In the summer of 2020, when we were protesting and marching for Black lives, we all put ourselves at risk of COVID-19. Yet at that moment, I realized that while COVID-19 was a threat, the bigger one, the one we continue to put band-aids on without real lasting and sustained reform, is racism. We had been here before with climate change, where band-aids were applied, the issue wholly ignored as the planet continued to heat up and natural disasters worsened.

This made me wonder if we had our priorities right and if COVID-19 simply illuminated just how wrong we have been?

However, while we are protesting, marching, and trying to live our fullest lives, we'll need to take care of ourselves. I've spent a lot of time—during a snapshot of time from February to June—exploring what that looks like from a COVID and mental health perspective. In this era, I've been proud to witness the numerous collaborations and partnerships people are making to help each other through these times. At the same time, I was completely enraged over the lack of empathy for our Black and Brown Americans, including those struggling with unemployment or loss. As a society, we are trying to live at the same pace amid a lack of resources and while balancing grief.

THE ETHICAL DILEMMA OF TRAVELING

With these two global crises in mind, is traveling around the country or globe being out of touch with reality, or is it something each of us should be able to do freely without guilt?

Alternatively, what are we to do about the island communities and countries whose economies rely heavily on tourism and have been devastated by the decrease in visitors?

While I was on a call with government officials from across the nation, it was interesting to hear their thoughts on tourism and travel.

"How will we know a place is safe to travel to and what kind of proof do we need to verify that? What happens if we see a resurgence or increase of cases as a result?"

Others would counter that we provide resources to mitigate the risks but that the economy is equally important.

"We need to open up the lines of tourism."

To answer this for myself, I thought about how various travel influencers responded in the wake of COVID-19 and our ensuing civil unrest. Social media influencers in other industries and sectors have had to adjust and change their approaches, going back to their roots to how they began traveling and connecting with audiences in the first place. During a time when influencers' main mode of content is unavailable to them, many have gotten creative by delving into other aspects of sharing the world, including recipes from other countries, virtual tours through pictures and videos of places visited in the past, as well as masterclasses to share strategies for connecting with a global audience.

Judy Kim, one such influencer from New York who focuses on food and fashion, notes that "the pandemic made [her] realize how unsustainable past work habits have been. [She] appreciates living slower and cooking [Korean] comfort food. . . while connecting with people globally."[153] This slower pace brings the same principles of the slow travel movement, which are key for taking the time to soak in a culture and appreciate it fully. COVID-19 forced us to slow down our rapid pace in traveling and illuminated the truth of how we were traveling unsustainably. While I had discovered this during my journey in the finding truth and open-mindedness mindset, these were brought to bear in how I would react and cope in a pandemic world.

On the other hand, those of us following various travel influencers have seen the nostalgic shots from past trips with a yearning to return to the shores of Greece or Bali. As quarantines and restrictions continued, these kinds of posts contradicted the public health messaging behind ceasing all nonessential travel. Several influencers chose not to comply for business or selfish reasons. Others posted here and there with their thoughts and plans for future travel, and once cases started steadying, went on road trips across the country. Yet one has to wonder if this is still the right move or way to use one's platform during a pandemic that still

---

153 Adrienne Jordan, "How COVID-19 Is Changing The Game For Travel Influencers," Forbes, Travel, June 9, 2020.

hasn't resolved, along with growing unrest in our country against racism.

For me, influencers I used to follow avidly have mostly been posting about mindfulness and mental health while taking risks to travel to each state amid rising cases. Another example includes posts I'll see about how we should travel to the Midwest or out west, and all I can think about is George Floyd. I also think about how every month since the protests in May, I've heard about a new unintended death, murder, or lynching across the US. There's no mention of these details in the post or even paying homage to the families suffering from these racist acts.

At a time when how one uses their platform matters, especially if they have a following of several hundred thousand, I'm really paying close attention to the content.

I'm certainly not at the status of travel influencer, but I do influence people to travel and experience other cultures. Because I know others are watching me, it motivates me to be more intentional about my reasons for taking that road trip or flight. I know if I had a following like the influencers do, I would use it to:

1. Promote safe traveling methods during COVID-19, and currently, our best weapons remain social distancing, handwashing, and mask-wearing, and quarantining if sick
2. Visit places that are devastated due to their heavy reliance on tourism, such as the US Virgin Islands or Hawaii and other Pacific Islands

3. Promote Black and Brown businesses that might be particularly hard hit to include following in the footsteps of Candacy Taylor's daring journey traveling to Green Book sites across America.

Do I miss traveling?

One hundred percent!

Every day, at least once, I think about the fact that if this was last year, I'd be on a plane or the open road heading somewhere new. At the same time, now didn't feel like the right time for me to focus on those desires.

I have several reasons why I reflected on my decision to stay grounded, despite the temptation to fly somewhere. I would take the occasional road trip to see family or a close friend after confirming they tested negative and had no symptoms, but in each of those trips, there were still inherent risks because of the nature of the virus. My reasons include:

1. Traveling is a privilege, not guaranteed, and not essential unless my work requires it to address COVID-19.
2. I can infect others without carrying symptoms, which can lead to death for the most vulnerable populations.
3. By traveling and infecting others who would then have to visit their health providers, I am stretching an already thin healthcare system.
4. After experiencing the loss of a family member this year and hearing stories from friends regarding their losses due to COVID-19 or complications from other conditions, the grief was too close to home for me to be that selfish.

Nevertheless, the advisement, while there are no effective vaccines and cures for those most vulnerable, is that nonessential travel should be limited.

In assessing your own willingness for risks and thinking about how we can combat the devastation to countries whose economies rely heavily on tourism, you'll have to come up with your own list of reasons or pros and cons. Of course, this should not replace the responsibility you have for doing your research to find the truth of whether traveling to a state or country is an option.

For these truths, the CDC and the US Department of State have compiled resources. Beyond those authoritative sources, several airline companies and flight search engines have included their own map or list of travel restrictions by location so you can always check on the status before planning a trip. Travel guidance was released by several travel companies and bloggers alike, changing as rapidly as the number of new cases each day as we learned more about the spread and impact of the disease in new places. Content released by the travel companies and influencers originally started with not flying to the most affected places, then to cheap flights to places deemed safe so as to combat the resulting economic losses, then to replacing flying with road trips in America, then to cautioning against road trips completely. Soon after, states issued out complete isolation via shelter in place orders as guidance while also closing borders or requiring quarantine. In these cases, the only traveling would be done in your backyard or in consuming content.

I will also be the first one to come forth and share where I was during that early period at the end of February when COVID-19 was still being assessed for its potential to spread globally.

* * *

At the end of February, I found myself on a beautiful walk, intentionally getting lost. Medellín was sunny and hilly, a direct contrast to the rest of Colombia as I looked out the flight window and saw most of the country enshrouded in rainclouds. That walk feels like a lifetime ago as I think about everything that follows and where I was a month after it happened.

We just learned how the people of Medellin overcame fear. Here I was testing my resilience amid keeping an eye out for the potential spread of the virus despite no new cases in South America yet. COVID was just beginning to worsen for America and the rest of the world as more countries joined the list of restrictions.

I could already see how much it was impacting the rest of our global economy and travel most of all. On the second day of my trip, I came into contact with someone else who had been exposed to a positive case, and even though we all took the necessary precautions, it reemphasized the risks of traveling in the current environment. Next, I came back from my trip and immediately got on a flight for a business day trip to Atlanta, Georgia. Later that day, I started feeling sick and was quarantined to my apartment just in case so as to not get anyone else sick. All these scares and potential possibilities of a viral outbreak prompted me to think about how the quick and silent spread of this virus had largely impacted travel.

While I can't confirm whether I had COVID-19, as I was unable to get tested, I did end up falling ill with an upper respiratory illness that I can only presume may have been the virus as I remained sick for over a month. That experience and the continued rise in cases was enough to keep me grounded for the rest of the year and away from the airports.

We must face the reality that traveling during COVID-19 will continue to be riddled with uncertainties before, during, and after the trip. In the months to follow, everyone I spoke to could think of an experience or tragedy related to COVID-19, which indicated how great of an impact the virus had on my circle of friends alone. Several said they had it or were exposed, while others knew someone else exposed or who died because of it. This was especially true for many in my network who were still traveling due to their jobs or for pleasure.

* * *

With restrictions on travel due to COVID-19, we have also achieved a lower collective global carbon footprint. This has resulted in a resurgence of animals taking back or taking over new habitats. For example, sea turtles are taking back beaches, lions in Kenya are reclaiming roads, and previously endangered species are repopulating.

I have to wonder where these animals will go when we return to these places? How will we decide where to go? How will we interact with these animals to cause the least disruption? These all remain part of the continued dialogue around the ethical dilemmas inherent with COVID-19 and any other future crises, including climate change.

While we had achieved two world-changing forces of reducing our carbon footprint and protecting wildlife and biodiversity, we were negatively impacting the other two of fueling local economies and promoting cultural awareness. Places that relied heavily on tourism were facing the double-edged sword of a pandemic along with a depressed economy. Local communities and businesses have been devastated, with many shutting down. Additionally, our awareness of other cultures is a risk in the wake of being unable to expose ourselves through our travels.

The industry continues to research, compile, and push out content related to safe and responsible travel. Much to my chagrin, these include topics related to sustainability.[154] This content, paired with my exploration of the sustainable travel mindsets, will prepare me to travel better once we can leave our homes with less risk to ourselves and others. It is my hope that the adoption of masks and sanitation practices we've learned will continue after COVID-19 as our global society won't soon forget the risks that we inherently faced with this pandemic. When looking at other countries that have woven mask-wearing into their daily lives, many were preceded by devastating epidemics.

---

154 Eric Weiner, "Travel Has Changed—So Must We," AFAR Magazine, September 17, 2020.

As nothing is guaranteed, a virus of this magnitude can strike again. These safe travel habits, paired with the enhanced sanitation and filtration systems that many in the aviation and transportation industry have adopted, will make up the future of our travel experiences. Finally, as people have been unable to travel abroad without risking quarantine, I've observed an increase in the number of road trips and RVs purchased for these overlanding excursions. A resurgence of backyard and local travel could mean that we have opportunities to implement the slow travel movement, practice gratitude, and reduce our carbon footprint.

While choosing my next trip has come with logistical challenges, it has also developed my ability to adapt and manage my expectations.

I have found that as of today, my safest options are walking or biking around my city, followed by driving. Given the uncertainty that COVID-19 has posed without a viable vaccine, traveling in enclosed spaces such as trains and planes are riskier options even with distancing because not every passenger complies with wearing a mask or keeping a safe distance. Perhaps this wariness will translate to the end of over-tourism and overcrowding, but for now, traveling solo or with a close group of friends and family who have tested negative is the most responsible way to move forward.

PART V

GIVING BACK

Be the change you wish to see in the world.

—MAHATMA GANDHI, LAWYER, POLITICIAN,
SOCIAL ACTIVIST, AND LEADER OF THE NATIONAL
MOVEMENT AGAINST BRITISH RULE OF INDIA.

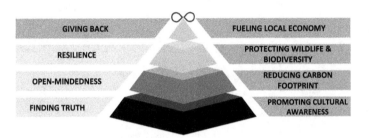

GIVING BACK		FUELING LOCAL ECONOMY
RESILIENCE		PROTECTING WILDLIFE & BIODIVERSITY
OPEN-MINDEDNESS		REDUCING CARBON FOOTPRINT
FINDING TRUTH		PROMOTING CULTURAL AWARENESS

Giving Back postures you to be more intentional on your travels. You will be inspired to identify the role you play in promoting the world-changing forces as a global activist or citizen.

CHAPTER 11

GLOBAL ACTIVIST— BE THE CHANGE YOU WISH TO SEE

BEFRIEND THE CHANGE: A GREAT GENERATION OF YOUNG ACTIVISTS

I breathe in the comforting smell of cardamom spice on my walk to Shilparamam, a craft village marketplace in Hyderabad, India. There, vendors sell clothes, spices, art, and other goods to locals and foreigners alike. I look around in amazement at the beauty and uniqueness of the saris worn by the women I encounter. I am there to barter for traditional saree cloth.

As I walk, I consider what beauty means in the context of Indian women. Looking around, I see Indian marketing ads and billboards with light-skinned Indian women. I also see ads with glamorous Bollywood actors and actresses promoting the Fair & Lovely skin brightening cream.

I look down at my chocolate Brown skin and realize my skin tone has gotten darker from the equatorial sun.

Growing up in Florida, I also used Fair & Lovely to lighten my skin, too. It was, after all, considered "the" beauty product of choice for Brown girls. Several beauty products that lightened skin tone claimed to have multi-vitamins that were good for the skin. In reality, products could also contain mercury or bleach, which, when applied to skin, can damage the cells and lead to discoloration.[155]

I'm revolted when I think about what generations of Brown girls who applied Fair & Lovely were doing to their bodies.

Throughout my life, I would often pass for North Indian, where the population is lighter than in the South. Comments about how my lighter skin was beautiful for a South Indian made me self-conscious about my skin color, especially when it would tan to a darker Brown. On that day in Hyderabad, however, it occurred to me as I walked toward the market that my tanned skin made me look South Indian.

In India, many believe that darker skin color equates to less beautiful, successful, or competent. Indians are beginning to examine and discuss colorism and the discrimination that many South Indian women faced due to their skin color. It's progress but far from sweeping change. In exploring how Black Lives Matter spurred Indians to address colorism, NPR reached out to several Indian women who are actively

155 Lauren Frayer, Black Lives Matter Gets Indians Talking About Skin Lightening And Colorism," NPR, July 9, 2020.

fighting the false narrative around darker skin. "Colorism is [problematic] . . . Darker-skinned Indians, especially women, face discrimination at work, at school — even in love [as] arranged marriage websites let families filter out by skin tone."[156]

On the road to Shilparamam, however, I embraced my darkened skin and my South Indian ancestors. The moment was symbolic for me because I felt like I was undoing years of putting on that lightening cream and damning the mentality that my lighter skin should be leveraged as clout for beauty and success. Nevertheless, I am aware of my light-skinned privileges, both in skin tone and in being half European. But I take pride in my South Indian heritage and it feels wrong for other Brown people to marvel at the privileges associated with my lighter side.

Who even decided that darker wasn't lovelier in the first place?

We bleached our skin in the name of beauty so that we could be Whiter or paler, but we were poisoning our minds and our bodies. Generations of Brown girls would remain insecure in their skin, perpetuating a mindset that darker-skinned people were not as valuable in our global society.

Twenty-two-year-old Chandana Hira, who called for reform when she initiated a petition against Fair & Lovely, faced similar challenges growing up. "I'm slightly dark," she said, "[but] I'd be called one of the dark-skinned people in [India]."[157] She

---

156 Ibid.
157 Ibid.

was not even a fraction darker than me and lighter than my South Indian cousins. While Chandana's work is not done, she has inspired other Indian activists as they lead their own movements to combat colorism in India, including Dark and Lovelier, Women of Worth, and Dark is Beautiful, to combat colorism in India.[158]

* * *

Growing up in an America and visiting an India where darker skin is frowned upon isn't an apt representation of the people of that country. When I look at who is making the decisions for us, I realize they don't look like us, and it makes sense why the policies, infrastructures, and systems don't work.

"It doesn't work for us."

In my conversations with Black and Brown people all over the world, this resounding fact continued to come up, indicating we weren't creating a sustainable lifestyle if not all humans can participate. It's unattainable, unsustainable, and further perpetuated in visiting other countries based on the centuries' old mindset that lighter is better.

There are times I am exhausted and nearly give up on this fight for a better future for us and a better world.

But I am reminded and fueled by my friendships with Black and Brown people all over the world that the long nights of

---

158 Ibid.

protesting and difficult conversations are necessary if we desire a more sustainable future where we can thrive, not just survive.

My support of Black Lives Matter is a demonstration of how I've befriended the change that our Black brothers and sisters are fighting for and how I am unwilling to be part of the status quo by staying silent.

I am proud to stand on the right side of history.

* * *

As I reflected on what it meant for me as a Brown person to stand with our Black brothers and sisters, the friendship of Martin Luther King, Jr. and Mohandas Gandhi came to mind. This reminded me of another young change-maker.

At the 2018 March for Our Lives in Washington, DC, I raised a fist in solidarity with Yolanda Renee King, granddaughter of Martin Luther King, Jr., as she proclaimed, "I have a dream that enough is enough . . . spread the word all across the nation, we are going to be a great generation."[159]

Every generation stands on the great shoulders of the generation who broke down barriers before us. Our generation looks to the nonviolent resistance movement led by Dr. King in 1960s America. And Dr. King found inspiration, it just so happens, in my father's native country of India.

---

159 Yolanda Renee King, "Yolanda Renee King, MLK's granddaughter: Enough is enough," CBS News, March 24, 2018, YouTube video, 1:57.

Mohandas Gandhi, one of India's most influential people, was an activist himself.[160] He protested against racism and apartheid in South Africa and fought colonial rule in India through nonviolent resistance.[161] Gandhi's approach inspired Martin Luther King, Jr. as King sought ways he could leave a lasting legacy through the Civil Rights Movement.

Martin Luther King, Jr. wrote in his essay "My Pilgrimage to Nonviolence" about how he was "fascinated by [Gandhi's] campaigns of nonviolent resistance . . . and the concept of Satyagraha, truth-force or love force. As [he] delved deeper into the philosophy of Gandhi [his] skepticism concerning the power of love gradually diminished, and [he] came to see . . . its potency a powerful and effective social force on a large scale. It was in this Gandhian emphasis on love and nonviolence" where King discovered an approach to the Civil Rights Movement in America.[162]

On one occasion, Martin Luther King Jr. took a trip to India to visit with his inspiration and documented observations in an essay on his Trip to the Land of Gandhi. He experienced the promise of international brotherhood and observed how ethnic and economic inequalities had a similar origin in racism.

---

160 "Gandhi, Mohandas," Martin Luther King, Jr. Encyclopedia, Stanford University, The Martin Luther King, Jr. Research and Education Institute, accessed on September 6, 2020.

161 Ibid.

162 Martin Luther King, Jr., "My Pilgrimage to Nonviolence," Fellowship 24 (September 1, 1958): 4–9.

Gandhi's nonviolence also applies the NVC principles of listening and communicating, which we learned about in our mindset on open-mindedness. King's open-mindedness to Gandhi's teachings and Gandhi's resilience to overcome the backlash he might face in challenging the status quo led both on an activism journey. Their mutual respect and friendship serve as a model for how to be an ally for movements that promote social justice.

What does it mean to be an ally? For me, this has meant taking the opportunity to:

- Stop and listen
- Educate myself and others
- Commit to action
- Celebrate the wins and self-care
- Repeat

With a bias toward action, I decided I would not only serve as an ally, but I would also be an activist at home and abroad.

* * *

As I desire to give back to the world this way, I take the time to find the truth behind global activism movements and to read about what a global activist is. One such discovery was Peter Weibel's Global activism: Art & Conflict in the twenty-first century, which explored how art as a medium for protesting.[163] In the book, global activism "describes and documents politically inspired global art practices that draw

---

163 Peter Weibel, Global activism: Art & Conflict in the 21st Century, 2018.

attention to grievances and demand the transformation of existing conditions through actions, demonstrations, and performances in public space."[164]

I applied this principle as I became involved in protests, petitions, marches, demonstrations, fundraisers, and collaborations with people around America.

I took risks to show up for our Black brothers and sisters because it was the right thing to do.

But the price of protesting is real, as I can attest.

I found myself relating all too well to the stories of demonstrators featured in Time magazine, who were either arrested or whose mental health was impacted to a point where they struggled to "get everything back on track . . . [their] confidence and faith . . . shattered."[165]

* * *

The third day of protests in Washington, DC brought more young people to the frontlines. Among the many young activists on Swann Street that Monday night in June was an incoming college freshman named Adam.

"This is so sad. This is wrong," he cried out.

---

164 Ibid.

165 Melissa Chan, "The Price of Protest," Time Magazine, Double Issue, September 21 and 28, 2020.

He's right.

I could see Adam shaking, with the tears falling down his face, and I went over to him to link arms in solidarity. I learned he aspired to become a computer engineer and had just graduated last weekend.

My heart broke to see this bright young person standing up for his beliefs and experiencing the trauma of unnecessary force from our police. Unfortunately, this is the reality that so many of our Black brothers and sisters face every day.

An influx of additional protestors joined us near the White House and then asked us to follow them through the streets of DC. I decided to keep marching.

Right before many of us were getting ready to go home, we got kettled or boxed in by police who labeled us peaceful protestors a threat while they sported riot gear and held their weapons at the ready. I never found out what happened to Adam as we were separated by police funneling minors in one direction and legal adults in another.

What would come to pass over the coming months following my protest experience in Washington, DC, in the wake of Floyd's death, likened a marathon. Between the tear gas, pepper spray, beating by police, and arrests with 200 other peaceful protestors for over twelve hours, it was clear to me that the other side wanted us to give up. Nevertheless, in those moments, we inspired one another in our bravery and courage.

Viral images of martial law on display at that night's protest sparked emotion around the world. The next night, the DC protest crowd grew by thousands, and the largest global movement for civil rights had begun. We, the youth, and your future were standing up for what we believed in.

It is this same courage I think of in another young activist whose unwavering voice continues to call out the inaction of global leaders to address climate change.

PROTECTING OUR HOME: ONCE YOU GO GREEN YOU NEVER GO BACK

Greta Thunberg's actions of sailing across the Atlantic and demanding real change to combat the effects of climate change caused more than a stir at the United Nations.[166] She had found a way to get their attention and grab a seat at the table. Her boldness made headlines and gave rise to a flight shaming movement that forced the travel industry to demonstrate a commitment to environmental sustainability.[167]

Greta serves as an inspiration to young people all over the world to be more conscious of their impacts, their purchases, and their habits. Following hers and other young activists' outcries against the system, young people began to challenge the status quo.

---

166 Greta Thunberg, "Greta Thunberg blasts world leaders: We will never forgive you," CBC News, streamed live on September 23, 2019, YouTube video, 4:28.

167 Ibid.

Greta's actions also inspired a new movement of sustainability activism among travel influencers. Manuel Bergmann was among them. Manuel, an Australian native and recent college graduate, headed to Bali and never looked back.

Bali stirs up images of swaying jungles of palm and bright blue waters surrounded by the most tropical arrangement of green you've ever seen. Perhaps you think of sandy white beaches.

Sorry to interrupt your picture postcard vacation, but this is not what Manuel Bergmann found when he visited the ocean and found himself wading through plastic and trash.

Manuel had a different kind of trip when he ventured out to the island country. Most of his time was spent learning about green initiatives, picking up trash, and working hard alongside the locals.[168]

How Manuel thought about traveling the world changed when he stepped foot in Bali's Green School, a wall-less bamboo campus set amid the lush green vegetation of the island jungle, which had originally opened in 2008. Several years later and Bergman's home base is still Bali, working as a sustainability activist contributing to antipollution efforts to conserve the oceans we play in when we visit the shores of Indonesia. Bergman decided he wanted to be part of the solution, not the problem. The first workshop he attended

---

168 "How to Cultivate Environmental Wellness and Zero Waste Living with Manuel Bergmann," May 31, 2019, Joy Energy Time, podcast, MP3 audio, 53:00.

taught him problem-solving strategies on how to live a more sustainable lifestyle, such as getting toward zero waste, refusing single-use straws, and not buying plastic bottles. "Step by step, I became more and more sustainable," Manuel stated, as he began to merge his passion for the environment with his love of travel.[169]

Manuel currently leverages his travel influence to share positive messages about the environment and spread awareness of the negative impacts of pollution, mistreatment of animals, and minimal reuse and recycling.[170]

The messages of activism are rooted in Gandhian ideology. Playing an active role in changing the world means leading by example to be the change we wish to see instead of waiting for someone else to take up the mantle.

Therefore, global activism can be used as a tool to educate and provide a path forward for how to sustain the world-changing forces of promoting wildlife and biodiversity, reducing our carbon footprint, promoting cultural awareness, and fueling the local economy.

169 Ibid.

170 "About Me," Coachingforcause, accessed on September 5, 2020.

CHAPTER 12

GLOBAL CITIZEN— YOUR ROLE IN SUSTAINABILITY

———

"Never doubt that a small group of thoughtful, committed citizens can change the world. Indeed, it is the only thing that ever has."[171]

While on a thought walk around my neighborhood to practice mindfulness, I passed one of our community libraries where I read this quote by cultural anthropologist Margaret Mead. Margaret's mother, a feminist political activist, inspired her to be an active citizen in America and abroad.[172] Margaret conducted expeditions to Samoa and New Guinea during her studies, which shaped her worldview on how the

---

171 "BookBrowse's Favorite Quotes," BookBrowse LLC, accessed on September 22, 2020.

172 Ibid.

power of mobilization and change starts at the grassroots level.[173]

I was immediately reminded of the actions other young activists and I took in DC to inspire change as we linked arms, each of us a critical component of the human chain to spark a chain reaction in the world. We showed up for each other by handing out food, water, and resources on legal support and healing services.

An age-old proverb, coined a mere decade after America's Declaration of Independence was signed, comes to mind when I think of our human chain.

"A chain is no stronger than its weakest link."[174]

The giving back mindset postures us to be responsible citizens in recognizing the ripple effects we have on others in the world. This mindset prepares us to engage in the world-changing forces which require each of us to give, whether through positive habits or giving up practices rooted in the problem. Each of us is a link in the same chain versus groups of people siloed by their borders and different practices. In reflecting on our humanity and our planet, I recognize we are not as strong or great as we can be.

---

173 Ibid.

174 Thomas Reid, "Essays on the intellectual powers of man," (Dublin, Printed for L. White, 1786), accessed on September 20, 2020.

Because of her experiences in Polynesia, Margaret postured herself as a global citizen and worked with other like-minded individuals to bring about change.[175]

What is a Global Citizen?

Upon looking for the answer, I came across the Global Poverty Project, an international education and campaigning nongovernmental organization (NGO) that created an international community known as the Global Citizen. The Global Citizen postures itself as "a movement of engaged citizens committed to defeating poverty, demanding equity, and defending the planet."[176]

The impact of the small actions of each committed citizen may not be immediately apparent. Still as they work together, they achieve great feats, influence world leaders, and contribute to shaping a better world for us.[177]

Well, these small actions added up.

To date, Global Citizen has tracked twenty-eight million actions taken and forty-eight billion dollars in commitments made.[178]

Still, there are organizations that pledge to eradicate the myriad of problems we face by fostering global citizenship.

---

175 "BookBrowse's Favorite Quotes," BookBrowse LLC.

176 "Citizenship," Global Citizen, accessed on September 20, 2020.

177 Ibid.

178 Ibid.

The UN Secretary General's Global Initiative on Education is one such organization that outlines how we must face global challenges by designing global solutions that have far-reaching changes informed by all human beings.[179]

To foster global citizenry, we must tackle the unequal world we live in, steeped in the ugly history of colonization, racism, and displacement. We must reverse the damages inflicted upon our planet from generations of inaction and ignorance. We must find ourselves and identify why we choose to travel, which requires that we be honest with ourselves, even if it's not comfortable finding out the truth about our privilege, inaction, or ignorance.

My first experience to serve as a committed citizen of my community involved volunteering. I thought about the power of giving time and talent for free and how meaningful that action is to the communities I help. I also considered that volunteering enables one way to easily exchange and share in cultural norms with the people you are helping. One of my most meaningful volunteer experiences includes developing the young minds of migrant children in India through teaching. I was giving back to my father's native country and bridging the gap between India and America through my actions.

---

179 "Priorities," United Nations Educational, Scientific, and Cultural Organization (UNESCO), accessed on September 20, 2020.

FOUR WORLD-CHANGING FORCES: A CIVIC DUTY

PROMOTING CULTURAL AWARENESS

Back in India, I walk along a dirt path, but instead of a craft village market, I head to the Aksharavani adaptive school for migrant children.[180]

As I approach the school, several dozen children shout in glee and run to greet us, their eyes hopeful, their smiles big. Every Tuesday and Thursday, I walk with four other study abroad students to Aksharavani to teach these children English and basic Math. The needs of these children highlight a gap in the education system and represent an opportunity for us to partner with teachers at our host institution, the University of Hyderabad, to foster change toward equal access to education.

Not only do we spend time teaching the children, but we also fundraise money to pay for the teachers who dedicate extra time outside their regular positions in the public schools. We learn about the significant challenges these children face when enrolling in the public school system. Their nomadic lifestyle also makes it difficult for them to permanently enroll in school because their parents search for work and move the family from place to place.

On our last day at the school, each child comes up to the front of the class and proudly recited to their peers and us everything they have learned over the past months. Most of

---

180 "Stories from the Site," Aksharavani, An Adaptive Community School in Hyderabad, India, accessed on September 5, 2020.

the students are able to recite numbers, the alphabet, and basic sentences in English.

This experience fosters a cultural and linguistic exchange as we speak both Hindi and English during our sessions with the children and share games. In five weeks, the small group of us students have accomplished meaningful change as we set the foundation for each child to explore a better future through education.

Unfortunately, it is impossible to know how their lives turned out. The school closed once the migrant families moved away due to the end of the temporary projects that had attracted them to this location in the first place.

I spoke to my Indian American friend Anusha who has always inspired me to give back with her yearly trips to Hyderabad, India, to volunteer. I learn about her process to engage the nonprofit and how she continues to sustain her commitment.

That sense of responsibility Anusha felt as she walked into the mud-brick home on a hot winter afternoon to see a group of girls playing and reading books would stay with her long after. It was her first time visiting Sheep NGOS Jeevodaya Home. When she left, she knew it wouldn't be the last time she would see those girls. Anusha saw herself in each beautiful Brown face and wanted to be a dream maker. These girls had come from poor and sometimes harsh beginnings. With access to education and a safe home, each girl would be able to pursue her dreams.

Anusha found ways to sustain her volunteer efforts and donations through her professional connections and networks. She was able to build the business case for supporting the Jeevodaya Home and pitch it to the company she worked for in America. Her appeals to corporate and social responsibility played to her favor as they selected the Jeevodaya Home as their charity of choice for the year. The businesses Anusha engaged to support also had the opportunity to learn more about India, including how nonprofit organizations addressed the country's greatest challenges. Anusha would also have the opportunity to continue to engage her colleagues and friends in a dialogue about her country.

Anusha actively bridged the gap between America and India by serving as a productive and contributing citizen to both.

Her story reminded me of the schoolchildren I had left behind. I knew that if I could return, I would find a way to build partnerships with organizations in America so we could sustain this important work in the future.

REDUCING CARBON FOOTPRINT

Is sustainable or green travel even feasible?

When in doubt, choose the Hogwarts Express Train.

I had been road tripping alone through Scotland's highlands and the Isle of Skye. These were long and winding roads through mountainous terrain, so naturally, the last few hours of my trip back to Edinburgh were exhausting. I had planned to catch a flight given their low cost and efficiency with time as I had wanted to spend a few more hours in London before my evening flight.

The blue-green numbers on my rental car dashboard flashed 3:30 a.m. I had about two hours left and figured I could afford a half-hour nap and still make it in time, so I drove into a pull-out area and leaned my seat back, preparing for a light snooze. Before you know it, I'm awakened by the distorted sound of a truck's horn some odd miles away and saw the time, a glaring 5:50 a.m. I woke with a start and realized I had definitely overslept, even though it was likely needed. I quickly looked up flights again since I had originally planned to catch one at nine in the morning. With dismay, I realized there were no other flights until late afternoon, which would be a risk to my international flight back home.

I thought and remembered something my free walking tour guide had said when I was in Edinburgh a few days ago.

"JK Rowling's Harry Potter was actually written right here in Edinburgh . . . the Hogwarts Express is based on when she used to take the train back to London for the weekend."

All of a sudden, what seemed like a disaster was a blessing in disguise as I realized I would love to experience what that was like, maybe feel the magic and inspiration this author did when she wrote easily one of my favorite book series of all time. I realized if I timed it right, I could make it back to London by lunchtime and still have about two hours to grab lunch in the market.

Renewed with this excitement, the two hours passed in the blink of an eye. I bought my train ticket, grabbed a veggie pie, and boarded my train within thirty minutes of departure. Even though it was a four-hour ride, it was a beautiful rendering of the Scottish and Northern England countryside. There were times the train passed by the ocean and other times through the middle of towns. I didn't realize I would enjoy a lengthy train ride this much, but it inspired me to be that much more adamant about exploring train travel in the future.

The next opportunity I had to test this out was on my way from Beijing, China to Hohhot, Inner Mongolia, my version of the Orient Express minus the plush red carpeting. While the train ride was long, the changing scenery through the mountains and grasslands was an exciting experience. While train travel may be comparable or more expensive than flying in some cases, in this instance, it was cheaper to take a train into Mongolia than to try to find a flight from America or elsewhere in Asia.

A serendipitous accident provided the opportunity I needed to put into practice traveling by rail versus air. Since that experience, I've often looked into whether a country has a rail option or what types of day trips or otherwise are available via rail. Furthermore, I've thought about traveling across America by rail and have found that Amtrak provides amenable options to include Wi-Fi, so you can even explore the possibility of a digital nomad life.

What if the train is not an option?

Are there any airlines we can feel comfortable taking knowing they are more fuel-efficient and living what they preach about sustainability? According to the International Council on Clean Transportation, there are several jet fuel-efficient airlines that have looked for ways to use less jet fuel, lower costs, and make planes lighter.[181]

- Alaska Airlines
- Frontier
- Spirit
- Hainan
- All Nippon Airways
- Norwegian Air Shuttle[182]

What about buying carbon offsets? Because carbon offsets are largely unregulated, it can be difficult to verify where and how your dollar is being used for a carbon offset project.

Patty, a leadership coach and world mountaineer, said it best when she firmly stated, "I'd rather plant my own damn trees than pay someone else. I do it right here in my yard."

Paying someone else to offset your emissions also doesn't change one's mindset.

It's better than nothing, but if you use it to offset every flight you are going on and still flying pretty regularly, this doesn't

---

181 Naya Olmer and Dan Rutherford, "US domestic airline fuel efficiency ranking, 2015–2016," The International Council on Clean Transportation, December 14, 2017.

182 Ibid.

compare to reducing your flight travel more significantly and/or choosing greener transit options, like trains. You are partly avoiding direct responsibility and awareness for your actions with a click of a button, a swipe of a card.

Living a greener lifestyle both at home and abroad can add up our collective actions to make a significant change. Regardless of the numbers, every small action toward the larger goals of sustainability, counts. Airbnb also explored greener ways for travel in their smart traveler series and suggested the following:

- putting your house to sleep by adjusting the thermostat, unplugging all electronics, using the water heater's vacation setting, and closing the curtains
- packing smarter with a goal of consuming less than the locals and an emphasis on recycling and reusability
- leaving no trace in parks, at the coast, or in a city
- if you must fly, choose fuel-efficient airlines
- engaging in your own carbon offsets, with more action required on your part[183]

FUELING LOCAL ECONOMY

Air travel continues to increase as the number of city pair connections increases. There are currently over 22,000 various cities paired through flights.[184]

---

183 Sarah Engler, "30 Ways to Travel with a Lighter Footprint," Airbnb Magazine, accessed on May 5, 2020.

184 2019 Aviation Benefits Report, Industry High-level Group (2020).

That's a lot of connections.

These connections make travel more accessible for people who live in various cities all over the world and creates opportunities for us to experience and interact with other citizens, where it may have been challenging otherwise.

This increase in city pair connections and cheaper flights also increases the trade in goods and services. This includes foreign investments that create sixty-five million jobs and contribute nearly three trillion to the global economy.[185]

While this represents the great economic impact of traveling, there are still conflicts to be aware of to ensure that you aren't fueling economies at the expense of our planet or a country's cultural norms. The sustainable travel mindsets were designed to keep these conflicts top of mind when engaging in the four world-changing forces, and this may mean reconciling those truths and giving back before arguing your case to support the business that is the travel industry.

During my road trips across America and on excursions abroad, I would visit local stores and markets to do my shopping. Looking at this as an investment in my wardrobe and other household goods I would need or use in my daily life, I was selective with what I bought. I walked around my apartment and realized how much had come from my trips. These mementos reminded me of the unique moments or experiences I had in each community or country and made me cherish those experiences even more.

---

185 Ibid.

- My sweaters came from Oregon, Mexico, Morocco, and Minnesota.
- My coasters came from four continents.
- My blankets came from Iceland and Nevada.
- My books came from Italy, Morocco, London, India, Australia, and more states than I can remember.

And of course, you can't forget the food. With food, I seek out the hole in the wall places instead of large national or international franchises. The more off the beaten path an eatery is, the more I like it.

Beyond the obvious benefits that come from buying keepsakes and cultural items is the experience itself. Walking through the marketplaces of each country feels like a scene out of a movie, as each stall reflects a grandeur which acts as a preview of the value you'll find if you stop at the stall, take a peek inside or engage with the vendor on its historical origins.

PROTECTING WILDLIFE AND BIODIVERSITY

Ensessa Kotteh means animal footprint in Amharic, the native language of Ethiopia, Africa. It is also the name of a wildlife reserve I visited in the country.

While in Ethiopia, I hoped to visit the Suba Menagesha Park and Forest and perhaps see some wildlife up close through a safari tour, not unlike the famously depicted safaris of Kenya and Tanzania. After an hour of driving and no clear route ahead, for I was unable to point out exactly where this was, and the driver was unfamiliar with the forest, we stopped to ask for directions from a few young men standing by a curbside in front of a gated entrance.

They, too, were unaware of how to get to this forest.

After a few more minutes of conversation with my driver, she turned around and told me these were workers at a wildlife conservation center, and while the place isn't open for visitors or tourists, they were happy to show me around. Unexpected and at once both honored and skeptical, I asked my driver if she felt it was safe. She nodded and said we could remain in the car as they opened the gate so that if at any point I didn't want to stay, we could leave. It took an immense amount of trust and open-mindedness to follow her and those young workers into the center that day, and as they opened the gates, I realized the leap of faith was completely worth it.

This detour led to a beautiful discovery of some of Ethiopia's most noble work as the center was also dedicated to saving animals from the harmful effects of humans.

I heard lions roaring, birds singing, cheetahs running behind the fence to keep up with the car, and at once, I wanted to stay the rest of the day. I wondered how common this was and marveled that were it not for the accident of getting lost on our way to the forest, I wouldn't even be able to share this story. The Ensessa Kotteh Wildlife Rescue, Conservation and Education Centre is also the first of its kind in the region.

I wasn't always aware of my responsibility to protect wildlife as I thought about my time in India again, where I had been riding on elephants blissfully ignorant of how this counters the majestic beast's ability to live freely in the wild. Instead, they are forced into a life of submitting to the whims of a tourist for long hours of rides. Once I found out the truth, I made a conscious choice not to ride another elephant and instead engage in activities that would safeguard and protect their way of life. My experience in Ethiopia was a peek into the window of what that could look like on other trips around the world, especially to places where exotic, endangered, and native animals roamed galore.

An unexpected detour in Ethiopia led to a responsible engagement with animals, which also upholds the world-changing force of protecting wildlife and biodiversity. This experience influenced me to be more intentional about my interactions with animals around the world. In this example, while I wasn't actively taking up the mantle toward animal rights because I had chosen to dedicate my energy toward anti-racism efforts, I was still able to find the truth and remain open-minded to exploring other options for animal experiences or encounters in different countries given this eye-opening experience.

RECOGNIZE GOOD INFLUENCE(R)S

Josephine Becker, founder of Treesnpeace, dedicates her actions to promote climate and social justice, and is one such example of a good influencer.[186] Josephine uses social media to post about living an eco-friendly lifestyle through low-carbon hobbies.

---

186 "Josephine of Treesnpeace," Ethical Influencers, accessed on September 20, 2020.

Implementing these hobbies requires a change from our normal way of consuming as much as we can during our travels. She shows how non-consumerist activities can be far from boring. She also emphasizes the communal aspect of many of the hobbies she has enacted and recommends others to spread the positive influence by involving friends, family, and locals.[187]

Several eco-friendly hobbies you can begin to employ in your own backyard include:

1. Spending more time outdoors and less time on our phones
2. Gardening
3. Repair, up-cycle, or donate clothes
4. Explore different options for food (various cuisines, traditions, or eating in more climate-friendly ways)
5. Volunteer for a good cause

Josephine picked up the hobby of tree identification and joining community forest walks to learn more about trees and the people walking through the forest with her. [188] Similar to the concept of forest bathing, which we explored in the finding truth mindset, Josephine was able to practice the giving back mindset by using these hobbies to actively reduce her footprint and protect biodiversity. She then used her social media influence to actively spread the message to others.

---

187 Ibid.
188 Ibid.

SOCIAL IMPACT

"I think we can achieve good and be profitable . . . add value and leave a place better," my African friend Mohammed (Mo) Kamara said as we spoke about sustainability and giving back to places through the guise of corporate responsibility and social impact.

Mo originally started giving back in other countries when he moved to America and went to New Jersey to help build houses with an angle toward teaching youth about Christianity. When he began to develop the business plan for his company, he wanted to primarily partner with an organization that was mission-driven and found Project Hope. He then proceeded to spend two to three weeks in various countries with a focus on strengthening health care systems. Mo ended up doing collaborations in Dominican Republic, Costa Rica, and Cuba. In this instance, social entrepreneurship drove his passions for traveling and engaging with people and businesses in other countries. But before coming in with his brand of solutions, Mo had to approach the locals with humility and a willingness to understand them before acting on his intentions.

Mo's experience represents a growing trend among young people entering the workforce today who wish to mix profitability with good. Additionally, many businesses are starting to explore corporate responsibility and sustainability more seriously. This is apparent in how businesses are hiring, reporting on, and investing in these areas more frequently. As I speak to other young professionals who wish to change the world, I believe this change can happen at both the grassroots local level and the top-most levels of industry.

* * *

As I explore my own power to create change through my actions, I have come to champion greener habits. While on my travels and at home, I continually practice recycling and reducing my consumption.

RECYCLING

I needed to take the time and effort to recycle more. I even took this to the extent of investing in a trash can that had a receptacle for both trash and recycling. In less than half a year, I noticed my personal practices changing measurably, to where my recycling output was larger than my trash or landfill contribution. I was turned onto the idea when I visited Vancouver, Canada, one New Years'. Even amid the masses of thousands of people, I could pick out from the crowd a group of young people in green shirts with tongs picking out trash from recycling and vice versa. As I approached the receptacle, I asked where to place each item I had, and they pointed out each bin (compost, landfill, recycling). I thanked them for doing this, amid the hectic buzz of people all around and on New Year's Eve, no less.

A young Canadian man said there's no other way I'd like to bring in 2019. He was making this a priority versus going out and spending that day like everyone else, not that there's anything wrong with that, but he clearly knew how he wanted to start out his year, aware that there would be many more moments of celebration and that this was one small way he could make a meaningful and (might I add) fairly significant impact. Imagine if that army of fifty volunteers weren't out that night what the streets of Vancouver would look like in the morning, not an uncommon sight in such a big city. I tried looking for whatever this initiative was online, but that's a needle in a haystack of data noise. It was impossible to find, so perhaps it really was an unorganized, informal group of young activists banding together for a cause. I thought to myself, things like this really ought to be highlighted, funded, and supported throughout the world.

REDUCING CONSUMPTION

I learned to pay closer attention to my habits around consumption and their impact on my carbon footprint. As I explored, I found more efficient and eco-friendly strategies to employ on my travels. I adapted to these changes by choosing different methods of transit, such as a train over a plane and exploring other accommodation options, such as camping. I also started packing lighter and carrying less baggage with me. I lived the reality of a backpacker, taking pride in being able to fit all of my necessities in a pack on my back. I became more mindful of what and where I was eating, taking a page out of Bourdain's book to try more hole in the wall places, which have often led to my favorite food experiences.

Being mindful of my consumption is most apparent on my camping and hiking trips. Not only am I challenging myself to extreme periods of physical activity and therefore am not prone to eat extremely large meals in the moment, but I'm also living much more off the earth when I'm camping in the desert or a yurt—an insulated tent—in the wilderness of the grasslands, seeking refuge under palm trees in the jungles and beaches of Hawaii, or setting up a tent in the forests surrounding some dramatic mountain range. I don't shy away from these humbling experiences and look at them as a way to embrace nature directly by using all my senses to take in the surrounding environment.

GLOBAL CITIZENSHIP: CONNECT TO YOUR ROOTS

For Black and Brown people in America, it can be challenging to feel at home. Our American citizenship is often wrought with historical inequalities from our inception to today. There are not many instances where one can maintain dual citizenship as countries tend to have stipulations in place for giving up one citizenship for theirs.

I decided I would find out what the process of obtaining dual or triple citizenship would entail. What I found was:

- Triple citizenship does not exist for my particular ethnic backgrounds.
- Dual citizenship with Hungary is possible through a lengthy application and interview with the Hungarian Embassy.
- Dual citizenship with India is not possible at this time.

While I have the privilege of knowing my ethnic roots, many of my Black friends whose ancestors were enslaved in America struggle to find their African roots through DNA testing, archive research, and stories.

Marking a promising year for Ghana, President Nana Addo Dankwa Akufo-Addo announced the Year of Return campaign in 2019. [189] Promoted as a homecoming for all people of African descent to gather within Ghana's borders, the campaign offered an opportunity to learn more about African culture and history. The campaign shed a spotlight on the allure of African destinations and culture to a wider global audience.

The Year of Return proved to be a year of returns on investment for Ghana. By attracting 1.5 billion visitors "home" to Ghana, the campaign injected more than one billion dollars into the country's economy. [190] The Ghanaian government also noted the year as a success because it drew positive attention to Ghana, including favorable content on the country and its culture, in international media reports. [191]

With this success in mind, the following year, Ghana announced the Beyond the Return campaign to engage Africans in the diaspora and people of African descent in trade and investing. [192] Beyond the Return sought to advance the connections between people across the diaspora for mutual benefit. Each would get to share in the growth and development of Africa while fostering trade relationships with Black Americans. [193] The Ghanaian President believes

---

189 Parker, Diakite, "How Ghana's Year Of Return Campaign Put Black Destinations In The Spotlight," Travel Noire, April 28, 2020.

190 Reality Check Team, "African diaspora: Did Ghana's Year of Return attract foreign visitors?" BBC News, January 30, 2020.

191 Ibid.

192 Parker, Diakite, "Ghana Launches 'Beyond The Return' Campaign," Travel Noire, January 5, 2020.

193 Ibid.

that the destiny of all Black people is bound with Africa. These campaigns help make Africa a place for progress and prosperity while combatting the false mirage that so many Ghanaian youths believe exists within a better life in Europe of America.[194]

∗ ∗ ∗

As a global citizen, you posture your habits and practices, both at home and abroad, to be sustainable so you are conserving what you need to for others around the world. We are a lot more connected in our impacts, and by taking responsible trips, we can live up to not taking more than we give.

At the end of each day, I am grateful we can still thrive on this planet despite our unsustainable practices. While we can't tackle every problem, if we work together, I guarantee we can leverage our collective action to help each other create and save that world we so enthusiastically want to roam through. I still pledge to uphold each world-changing force through my small and purposeful actions.

To date, these small actions include changing or adopting different hobbies on my travels, such as volunteering in the community, visiting wildlife conservation centers instead of zoos, buying at local markets instead of malls, and traveling by train instead of a plane.

---

194 Ibid.

PART VI

TO INFINITY
AND BEYOND

*A journey to the center of the Earth brings
images of a fire in the hearth. When you
reflect on your journey towards sustainability,
remember that it's a love story.*

—PRIYANKA SURIO, AUTHOR, THIRD
CULTURE KIDS OF THE WORLD

Infinity applies everything we've learned to a future of travel
that should be sustainable and better for the world. As a call
to action, you will take the global citizen pledge to uphold
the world-changing forces. Through love, leave no human or
creature behind as we move to infinity and beyond.

CHAPTER 13

THE FUTURE OF TRAVEL IN A THIRD CULTURE WORLD

THIRD CULTURE WORLD

While the future holds much promise for building smarter cities, faster trains, and deeper exploration opportunities in space for citizens, it also begs the question of how sustainable that is from a few lenses.

- Are we moving too fast?
- Is this type of travel and rebuilding of our infrastructures harmful to our planet?
- Would everyone have the opportunity to benefit from investments in these areas?
- How will this address the myriad of problems we currently face and the world-changing forces that still need addressing?

We should maintain a healthy skepticism for exploration for the sake of exploration in our consideration of sustainable travel. As we enter an increasingly globalized world that will result in more third culture kids (TCKs), how will those of us who are TCKs use our unique perspectives to bridge cultures?

Even if you are not a TCK, you can still play a role in bridge-building by posturing yourself as a global citizen. Rooted in the sustainable travel mindsets, global citizens have the opportunity to usher positive world-changing forces that connect the world and make it a safer and better place for all to live in. Many of us are already taking the first step as we take the time to plan our first or hundredth trip in an age of significant global change and crisis. When we apply the mindsets to our travels, we are creating a better world for all of us, instead of a temporary vacation for one or a few.

Five months after that fateful night at BLM Plaza marked the day Americans would have an opportunity to fulfill their civic duty and vote. As I walked through the plaza, I felt a catharsis and emotion at how much transpired on those streets leading up to the White House and how the nature of this place changed. As I walked around, I heard people arguing about the election and who was better suited to lead our country. In my mind, there was no debate as my cause was about removing any trace of racism wherever, and however, it may exist. With that strongly etched in my mind, I felt moved to join other Americans who were holding up a black tarp with large white letters stating in all caps, REMOVE TRUMP.

Afterward, I continued walking. I noticed the anticipation around me from people watching the election results live on a screen in the middle of a nearby park, and as a group of young street dancers encouraged the audience to dance to the beat of the music as it reverberated off of the buildings. Amid all of this, stationed at each corner were cop cars, watching like vultures at the ensuing mix of humans gathered in the plaza awaiting the fate of a country.

A few days later, on a bright November Saturday, the roar is palpable as the announcement came of the forty-sixth president-elect.

Joe Biden and Kamala Devi Harris represent a new direction for the future of a divided America, one that seeks to build bridges instead of walls.[195]

In a statement, President-Elect Biden speaks to unity as he calls on the nation to set aside our differences. "It's time for America to unite. And to heal . . . to put the anger and harsh rhetoric behind us and come together as a nation."[196]

Thousands of people from all diverse backgrounds flood the streets of DC, making their way with joyous cacophony to Black Lives Matter Plaza.

After months of protesting against racism at the plaza, it is time to celebrate.

"You are fired . . . duh, duh, duh, duh, duh."

---

195 Jonathan Lemire and Zeke Miller, "Biden wins White House, vowing new direction for divided US," Associated Press, November 7, 2020.

196 Ibid.

The crowd's echoes carry throughout the city as people dance, spray paint art, sing, blow horns, and gather in front of the White House. We have come full circle, like an infinity, spreading a message of love instead of hate for our people.

Like the plaza, America is changing because of people like myself and people like Kamala.

As we express excitement on the streets of DC, this moment changes history once more as Kamala is the first Black woman and Indian American to become vice president.

That's right. Kamala is also a TCK as her mother is from India and her father is from Jamaica. Kamala also hails from a lineage of activists as her mother and father were actively engaged in civil rights movements during their time in college, and Kamala's maternal grandfather was a political activist in India. It's no surprise then that she reflects the America other TCKs and I envision.

TCKs don't fit neatly into Black or White.

We're mixtures of something entirely new, and we're here to tell you that the status quo doesn't work for us.

I call upon all TCKs to weave in the aspects of being multinational into how we lead through this change in America because we are that change. What traditions or beliefs will we choose to uphold from our various homes, and how will we share those with America? If we are indeed the melting pot, it's time to see what the experiment of globalization yields.

TCKs can pave the way for an entirely new concept, the third culture world (TCW).

While some of us may be tempted to leave the country or join the expat community, I believe we have a larger duty to save this place for ourselves and future multinationals to the extent we wish to call America home. Perhaps, some of us will find that calling in one of the other countries we have a connection or call home. I encourage each of us to think about how we will serve as the bridge-makers between our respective countries.

A TCW not only boasts a diverse and mixed ethnic composition of its people, but it also promotes international relationships as we bring countries together to engage in a third place without strife or misunderstanding. This is similar to the concept of a third place, which offers a different atmosphere or home away from home. We have always felt this way in our very existence and have learned to embrace it and continue to embrace it as we announce our respective identities like Lupita and Hasan did. Most places fall within the confines of a box, like the Black or White concept, because TCKs color outside the lines with our very existence, the creation of a TCW can spur innovation in how we collectively and collaboratively work toward a more diverse and inclusive future.

USING TECHNOLOGY TO BUILD CITIES OF THE FUTURE

Pop. Crack. A young Nunatsiavut Inuit woman living in Nunavut, Canada, frowns as she anxiously listens to a sound like light thunder reverberating through the air, a sign of glacial ice melting into the Arctic Ocean. The changing climate conditions and resulting environmental impacts run deeper than the surface of our polar caps, extending to the health and wellbeing of Arctic communities in the rural frontier regions. With the increased prevalence and severity of extreme weather events, changes in sea ice resulting in water and food insecurity, and the already limited social and physical infrastructure, many of these populations face multiple threats. The opportunity to innovate and rebuild the infrastructure of cities around the world to thrive in the late twenty-first century is prime. In this way, technology, when used for good, is one method by which we can achieve this.

From technology, we can learn more about the risks that remote communities face, to include preserving and sharing their cultures. Technology acts as a bridge to more sustainable travel, cities, and lifestyles. In thinking about technology's impact on the future of travel, we can use it to:

- Expand on the opportunity the COVID-19 pandemic has created through increased virtual experiences
- Strengthen vulnerable communities and design cities of the future through a concept known as smart cities
- Explore how faster transportation options can reduce our carbon footprint and the time it takes to get to places

VIRTUAL TRAVEL EXPERIENCES

While not a replacement for in-person experiences and human connection, technology in the form of streaming videos, websites, and interactive engaging photos can still offer a perspective of other places. By sharing their culture, their history, and their food, the world has an opportunity to learn about these places without traveling to them. There are a number of current virtual opportunities to explore various countries that I think can and should extend to places beyond those on the travel industry's Top 100 list so that we can uncover the truths of these lesser-known places and people.

First, I sought out to define what a virtual experience was, what were its respective elements, what makes them different from the content we already have on social media platforms in the form of videos and pictures, and is this something that the everyday traveler can implement in partnership with a community. I wanted to explore how we could do more of these whenever and wherever we might be traveling in a way that's not only culturally appropriate and respectful, but also brings attention to those communities we are highlighting. Virtual experiences could boost countries' economies, tourism, and recognition in the world.

Virtual experiences consist of several elements, including:

1. A place that usually requires an entrance fee or monetary contribution like a museum or most national parks
2. Hikes where most of the experience usually happens on the trail and can't be fully captured through pictures of the main attractions (mountain peak, waterfall, valley)
3. A band of sand bandits playing their native Berber music and sharing that over WhatsApp—musical experiences in general that are live-streamed (e.g., Global Citizen's music festivals and benefits concerts)

Since COVID-19, digital creative and travel companies have banded together with organizations like the US National Park Service to increase the amount of virtual access and content we have on places around the world during the coronavirus pandemic. It changed the industry in the interim, but it made me question why we haven't been and why we can't do this more often through the right collaborations and partnerships, and for places that are more remote or for which using technology in this way is difficult, what can we do as travelers to elevate and highlight that place beyond our pictures and words?

SMART CITIES AND COMMUNITIES

What if we could have not only smarter travelers but also smarter cities that could contribute to our collective advancement as a human race?

As the body of knowledge is still growing, several pilot implementations and definitions of what smart cities entail, have emerged. The work of Chris Gibbons, CEO of the Greystone Group, has unearthed a different definition where residents of the smart community engage with smart services, often through a digital ecosystem, designed to improve their health.[197]

The global nonprofit Health Information Management and Systems Society (HIMSS) has defined smart communities as an accelerator of government modernization and innovation

---

197 Chris, Gibbons, "What do Smart Cities have to do with Interoperability?" December 13, 2019.

by leveraging public-private partnerships to address population and wellness goals through trusted, secure, and innovative technologies. Smart cities focus on transportation, infrastructure, city lighting, and government services.[198] Smart technologies include sensors that can detect certain physical or biological changes.[199]

Smart cities also rely on integrating health-related data across various sectors of health and human services, transportation, housing, and environmental health.[200] Ensuring the systems are connected and can talk to one another better informs those designing these smart systems to do so with a greater understanding of what kinds of policies and practices will drive toward improved health outcomes for the most emerging deadly health threats. Smart cities can also generate revenue through user fees, subscriptions, advertising, and other business models.

If such a system were in place in the most vulnerable communities, including the remote regions of the Arctic, for example, it would promote wellness in the absence of access to proper healthcare through the use of digital health services and applications while also engaging citizens in proactively tracking changes to their climate to inform preparedness and mitigation strategies well in advance.

---

198 Health Capital Helsinki. "HIMSS Webinar: Smart Communities & Cities
    - cases from Finland." Accessed on January 21, 2020.

199 Ibid.

200 Ibid.

There are several examples in practice, including the Arctic country of Finland, a large country with some of the longest distances between cities. One such example is the Get Home Safety project in the community of Jatkasaari, Finland, where the Internet of Things (IoT) is linking street lighting in various geographic locations with sensor technology to ensure residents who walk in these areas can feel safe or get home safely amid the darkness of winter.[201] Finland has taken steps toward carbon neutrality and energy efficiency using the same technologies to make smarter decisions, too.

While there is still much to be explored and desired as it relates to expanding the concept of smart cities and communities, the initial work in Finland will serve as a blueprint for what's possible in its Arctic regions and provide opportunities to translate these promising practices to other countries like Alaska in the United States or Nunavut in Canada. Key to Finland's early success was an investment from the government, matched with the technology and expertise of private companies.

I envisioned this future as I prepared for an early Thursday morning call with a group of Finland's finest researchers, practitioners, and technologists.

After my exposure to Alaska, I ended up revisiting Iceland and then traveling to Chile, Norway, and Scotland, because I wanted to see the polar regions and experience climate change firsthand. While it has always been a dream of mine to visit faraway places such as the Arctic (e.g., Greenland,

---

201 Ibid.

Finland) and Antarctica, I didn't wish to do so at the expense of the place itself. I believe there had to be a balance, and the creation of more airports across Greenland or more cruises to Antarctica so as to increase access and open tourism routes to each place was full of pros and cons that I was still weighing.

Fast-forward to my call with colleagues in Finland, where I discussed how I could meaningfully give back or contribute to making a lasting, positive impact in the Arctic beyond the self-serving aspects of tourism. I conducted research on smart cities and the unique challenges of the Arctic. I then designed a project to explore the feasibility of building a foundation for smart Arctic communities in Finland by using technology and digital solutions to improve the communities' ability to track and monitor their wellness habits, which would also consider their environment's conduciveness for healthy options. In addition to research, I would need resources, so I explored various scholarship or fellowship opportunities similar to what I had explored for my trip to India, which remains my longest experience outside of America.

Discovering the Fulbright Arctic scholarship opportunity, I began to prepare my materials and design a future where I could contribute to these Arctic communities in an innovative way. I secured an international institutional partner who would collaborate with me to implement the project for up to three months. The scholarship itself would support transit, time dedicated to conducting research and implementing the project, and living expenses.

The commitment from my international partners in Finland would only require a few hours in the coming months to scope out the project, and then several hours over the course of the three months dedicated to the project to collaborate and share findings. I was also charged with disseminating findings upon my return back home to America, specifically Alaska, as the only state in the Arctic, for the purpose of informing their own strategies to build smarter cities and to further strengthen the relationships between Finland and Alaska's Arctic communities.

While the Arctic might appear a faraway starting place for rebuilding the bridges across our world, the community of practitioners that conduct work in our polar regions is one of the most international and diverse groups of people. This global community unites around a common goal as the Arctic spans multiple countries and does not see borders when faced with the most dramatic effects of climate change.

Additionally, the Arctic regions have long learned about the devastation of climate change on their way of life. People who live here had to test and innovate solutions to combat the devastation of climate change from sea levels rising to glacial ice melting to the emergence of bacteria previously trapped in ice, which impacts food supply and human health. We can learn from the polar regions as we think about how we will prepare for and mitigate the disastrous effects of climate change in our own backyards.

We are already creating an infrastructure for sustainable methods of transportation by reducing time and fuel efficiency while increasing accessibility and comfort. One example is the continued development of bullet trains all over the world, and which has been implemented successfully in East Asia.

FROM EXPRESS TO BULLET TRAIN

Tokaido Shinkansen. There it was, and then it was gone in the blink of an eye, moving so fast it was scary.

You see it coming around the bend, and you've heard that it's among the fastest trains in the world, like a plane running at the full force of 300 kilometers per hour.

If you haven't overcome your fears yet, I encourage you to spend more time in chapter nine in the resilience mindset and take pride in it. After all, I encourage you to enjoy the journey and not rush into a future end state, where you may unhappily reach the top of Maslow's Hierarchy too soon or burn out as I did and seek escape through travel or other things far less enriching.

Despite what it looks like in videos, real-life, or your imagination (trust me, they all differ), the Shinkansen is one of the smoothest rides I've ever experienced. Eclipsed only slightly by their East Asian neighbor in Shanghai, China at 380 kilometers per hour, the Maglev Train founded in 2004 became the world's first commercially operated bullet train and continues to take the top spot with trains hitting speeds of 431 kilometers.[202]

---

202 "China Train Types," Shanghai Highlights, accessed July 14, 2020.

AN EXISTENTIAL QUESTION—SPACE TOURISM?

Patty nostalgically reminisced, "I would have loved to be an astronaut. They are the true travelers going into the unknown. Sometimes I seek to be surprised by what's not known a new path."

I decided to explore what astronauts truly thought about traveling, including space travel.

A handful of private citizens have already been there with the wealthiest of those on Earth who have spent twenty to forty million on the endeavor. Many private companies are working to develop space tourism programs and out-of-this-world experiences, including Virgin Galactic, Blue Origin, and SpaceX. These private companies provide opportunities to experience everything from weightlessness to rocket ship rides and are designing stays at future luxury hotels in space.

One astronaut believes that if people were able to view the Earth from that perspective, they would have more appreciation for the collective of humanity. "I seriously believe that if more people had the opportunity to go into space and see the Earth from that vantage point, they would definitely stop thinking of themselves as being from this country or that country and slowly start feeling like they're just from this planet," said Anna Fisher, one of the original six women accepted to NASA's astronaut training program.[203]

---

203 Harriet Baskas, "Nine Travel Tips from Astronauts," Smithsonian Magazine, August 9, 2018.

While I agree with this sentiment, I was skeptical about the feasibility of this and whether we would see this happen within our lifetime.

A month after the May 30, 2020, SpaceX launch of two private citizens into earth's orbit, I learned of another initiative to invigorate space exploration.[204]

What a time to be alive, summer 2020, right in the middle of a global pandemic seeing a rise in cases in several states and amid racial tensions triggered by the senseless killing of Black men and women.

In my opinion, the launch and subsequent advancements seemed out of touch with what was happening on earth. Perhaps it was the ultimate escape, or the bigger picture intended to create hope and fuel opportunities for a new generation of Black and Brown astronauts. This is assuming they make it out of the trauma and chaos down on earth.

Of all federally funded agencies or initiatives, NASA's STEM diversity and pipeline programs are the most robust. I recall looking at their various programs as a model on one of my federal consulting projects to create a STEM diversity strategic plan. So, of course, I wasn't surprised when I learned that NASA's Kennedy Space Center in Florida and Johnson Space Center in Texas had respectively joined forces to advance the gold standard of space tourism by signing Space Act Agreements with spaceflight companies SpaceX to design

---

204 "NASA Astronauts Launch from America in Historic Test Flight of SpaceX Crew Dragon," NASA, May 30, 2020.

a twenty-first century spaceport and with Virgin Galactic to develop a private orbital astronaut readiness program.[205]

The goal of this initiative aligns with NASA's plan to increase the commercial use of their International Space Station (ISS). However, the partnership outlines that candidates will be those interested in purchasing private astronaut missions to ISS, which will include training and transportation, support, and coordination using space station resources, but also includes a hefty and mostly unattainable price tag for the average citizen. Yet both NASA and Virgin Galactic remain optimistic that this is a catalyst for innovation and leads for a more positive future.

So, what can we learn from these out-of-this-world travelers?

The Smithsonian asked this same question and reached out to several astronauts about their travel tips and guidance. Preparation starts with finding and understanding yourself and then doing your research. "Use a checklist," advises Frederick "Rick" Hauck, a former NASA astronaut who piloted and commanded several Space Shuttle missions, "There are many endeavors in this world that would be much better executed if people kept checklists. I have one I refer to every time I travel."[206] Also, packing lightly and being open-minded are key strategies astronauts have employed. Astronauts overcome fear in preparation for their strenuous and risky journey outside of our planet through constant practice.

---

205 "Current Space Act Agreements," NASA, last updated October 5, 2020.
206 Harriet Baskas, "Nine Travel Tips from Astronauts."

Beyond the training inherent in their preparation, they also practice mindfulness, a skill we learned was important in the finding truth mindset. Many believe in the value of appreciating the moment and getting a new perspective about yourself by remaining open, which can happen anywhere on earth or in outer space.

"You can go three miles down the road, go to the top of a building, get on a boat or an airplane and get a new perspective on who you are," said Astronaut Stott, who is disappointed when she sees fellow airplane passengers go straight to watching a movie, to work or to sleep.[207]

"It's important to be awake and experience the journey," said Stott, "and to be surprised by what you see and feel along the way."[208]

Of course, flight travel requires billions of dollars, heavy machinery, and tons of fuel, making it the least efficient option at the moment.[209]

"There can never be a perfect machine in space; every design has a trade-off."[210] Designers will always have to sacrifice something with space transit, whether it be fuel efficiency, time, performance, safety, or another metric.[211]

---

207 Ibid.

208 Ibid.

209 Ibid.

210 Ibid.

211 Ibid.

Because safety is so elemental, it would be vital to understand what we are trading off and whether that's feasible for space flight. Hadfield uses the space shuttle as an example. The shuttle has wings and a large payload bay, which allows it to bring satellites into space and return them home. It can also carry large facilities such as Spacelab, a reusable scientific laboratory. But the design also complicates reentry and carries risks for manual flight.[212]

As more people continue to be interested in space travel, and private citizens are boarding space missions and flights to outer orbit, it stands to reason that space tourism will emerge much like how air travel has. Currently, space travel is only accessible to the extremely wealthy and trained astronauts, but like the flight industry, prices will eventually stabilize as it becomes more feasible and efficient to travel beyond our atmosphere, thus being a potential option for citizens who desire such an experience. Of course, the drawbacks to space travel are apparent in several renditions that we've seen throughout history and depicted in our entertainment industry through movies like 2001: *A Space Odyssey, Lucy in the Sky,* and *Ad Astra,* which all explore the deep-rooted psychological impacts of space travel.[213]

The wonder of space couldn't be eclipsed by the immense isolation that one could feel overlooking the blue mass that

---

212 Ibid.

213 Chris Klimek, "With the New Movie Ad Astra, James Gray and Brad Pitt Offer a "Plausible" Vision of Late-21st Century Space Travel," Air & Space Magazine, Smithsonian Institution, September 20, 2019.

is our planet, realizing just how small we are and how far away one is from everything humans know.

What haunts me about Lucy's journey is that post-mission, she became fixated on space to such an extent that she lost touch with reality. In the movie, Lucy used her fervor for space missions and training as an unhealthy way to escape the immense unhappiness, lack of fulfillment, and self-imposed boredom she felt from her life.

Lucy's journey loosely reminded me of the unhealthy ways I had previously approached traveling as an escape more than a privilege. Ultimately, what brought about Lucy's downfall was a romantic relationship she got wrapped up in as another form of escape and validation. Similarly, in Ad Astra, there are depictions of a robotic machine conducting a mental health screening at the end of every major action, decision, or mission, and in some cases withholding information from our main protagonist.[214]

In Ad Astra, the filmmakers created their vision of the technical, commercial, and political realities of what space travel might develop into by the late twenty-first century. The first space mission in the movie is to the moon, aligning with NASA's current lunar initiatives as part of their Artemis program, which aims to return astronauts to the surface by 2024. In the movie, Virgin Atlantic flights to the moon bring tourists to what appears to be more of a theme park, rife with chain restaurants and souvenir shops.[215] The movie explores

214 Ibid.

215 Ibid.

the concept of territorial boundaries and borders when the crew is traveling across the surface and raided by pirates contesting and exerting their dominance over some of the moon's regions and natural resources.[216]

Similarly, there continues to be turf wars over Antarctica and Greenland in terms of the potential crude oil resources underneath the polar ice caps and the monetization of tourism. While these turf wars can continue to sow seeds of discord instead of unity, they also threaten the climate and exacerbate the effects of global warming. I caution that we shouldn't embark on new discoveries and explorations without solving our problems on earth first.

If we can pour billions of dollars into something that only benefits a few humans, I don't see us achieving a TCW. Advancements in space travel that serve to benefit the powerful or privileged continue to perpetuate an unequal world and may have additional implications for climate change. I can envision a future in which we create more of the same, only with the added complication of outer space. And more of the same, amid the world's industrial and technological revolutions, led to our current state of affairs.

There is enough meaningful work to embark on here on planet earth that can use the resources and intelligence that make up space exploration and travel. Furthermore, I would call upon our space exploration industry to use their discoveries, technological advancements, and capabilities to

---

216 Ibid.

support sustainable travel and address the four world-changing forces instead.

CHAPTER 14

GLOBAL CITIZEN PLEDGE

—

Now that our winding journey up and down a pyramid of mindsets has illuminated your path to sustainability, you're better prepared to start your traveling journey. You've taken time to pause at the end of each chapter to mindfully reflect on where to focus most acutely. You've learned you don't have to be a third culture kid (TCK) or even hold dual or multiple citizenships to consider yourself a global citizen. Now it's time to put the suggestions and strategies in this book into practice.

I created a call to action out of love for our world and each of you as future global citizens to use as an anthem. You can take this anthem with you on future travels and revisit it time and again. I thought about creating a pledge or a mantra of positive affirmations that I might practice with mindfulness. I reflected on past pledges I had committed to, like my own country's Pledge of Allegiance.

To bring about the change I wish to see in the world, I decided a pledge was most appropriate as a promise or agreement to do a specific action.[217]

In thinking through the pledge, I looked at several previous examples that I thought might serve as good models for us as we venture into the world as sustainable travelers ushering in the world-changing forces.

I took a page out of Shirley Williams' writings with her composition of "The Black Child's Pledge," published in the Black Panther newsletter in 1968.[218] The pledge highlights the Panthers' militancy and Black-nationalist outlook while emphasizing the importance of education, physical fitness, abstinence from drugs and their respective influencers, community solidarity, and collaboration among Black children. Black history is American history, and as such, we must recognize the original TCKs of America were from Africa and had to adapt to the situations forced upon them. Williams' answer to this was to create a pledge for Black people to each other in the name of unity.[219] This represents a powerful message for a people that have generations of separation from country, culture, and each other.

I developed the Global Citizen Pledge from the idea that we are pledging to each other—all nationalities and backgrounds around the world—in the name of sustainability.

---

217 Encyclopedia Britannica Online. s.v. "pledge," accessed September 3, 2020.

218 Shirley Williams, "The Black Child's Pledge," HERB: Resources for Teachers, accessed June 22, 2020.

219 Ibid.

I also knew the pledge needed to include the four world-changing forces and needed to find examples of pledges to the environment. When I first happened upon Leave No Trace Behind, I had been trekking in a national park. As I came to learn more about the sustainable and environmentally friendly lifestyle they promoted through their seven principles, I knew that weaving in aspects of their commitment to the environment would be important to embed in the pledge.[220]

When we are on that rocky road toward resilience, it helps to know we are not alone. Each of us can motivate and inspire our fellow travelers along their sustainability journey. And because we can, we should. When author Cheryl Strayed solo-hiked the Pacific Crest Trail (PCT) in her mid-20s, she was ill-prepared for the challenging terrain. And yet, even as an inexperienced hiker, Cheryl managed to motivate and inspire not only hikers she encountered on the trail but also those who'd follow behind her. At each PCT checkpoint, hikers sign a logbook, and many choose to write an adage, a short story, a line of gratitude, a doodle, or a memento. Cheryl, a gifted writer, left poems in the logbooks, each of them a lyrical reminder of the beauty in life's simplest things. The raw, real emotion in her writing inspired me to capture my own emotion just as openly and honestly in the pledge as Cheryl did in the poetry she left behind on the PCT.

Next, I revisited the language and research used to develop sustainable travel mindsets. As I combed through the

---

220 The Seven Principles," Leave No Trace, Center for Outdoor Ethics, Accessed September 5, 2020.

initiatives the travel industry and key travel influencers have framed around sustainability, racism, and climate change, some interesting trends emerged. I applied my qualitative analytical skills to curate the most common words I came across and wove aspects of them into the pledge.

- local experiences
- authenticity
- sustainability
- reducing impact to global warming
- preparing for climate change
- global economy
- carbon offsetting, or a lower carbon-economy
- staying silent as a failure
- commitment to racial justice
- systemic change
- self-reflection
- checking biases and privilege

GLOBAL CITIZEN PLEDGE

After you review the pledge, you may have your own thoughts based on your unique travel experiences. I encourage you to adapt, create, and make this pledge your own as you commit to:

1. act more sustainably when you travel
2. embrace cultures of the world as a global citizen

Global Citizen Pledge

First, I take a breath and then tune into my surroundings while in self-reflection. **I pledge to be mindful.**

I recognize what motivates my journey to this place. My motivations do not harm the people or the planet. **I pledge to always find out the truth**, which may include the occasional or frequent checking of my privilege, bias, or blessings.

I notice the people, the culture, the creatures, and the environment, and my role in this unfolding story at this moment in time. **I pledge to be open-minded.**

I understand that if I wish to enrich my experience and make a lasting, authentic connection, I must love these people as they are without judgment and embrace their culture in the way it's meant to be, so long as I'm not harming myself or compromising my beliefs in the process. And if something comes across my path that conflicts with or challenges my beliefs, I'll remember my pledge to be open-minded.

I know this journey will be a roller coaster of emotions and experiences on the best of days. I also know that I may not always know better and accept the unfortunate reality of not acting better as a result. I pledge to forgive myself and others for our ignorance. I pledge to overcome my fear of challenging myself to change for the better. In my personal growth, **I pledge to be resilient.**

If I have doubts, I begin with love, first for myself, and then once I know this, love for others. **I pledge to love and promote all cultures**, for they are significant in our collective human history or humanstry.

Parallel to this, **I pledge to fight for those communities that still face an unequal world every day and to give back** whenever and however I can.

I take the time to slow down and explore the sustainable travel mindsets. I know that my travels will become more sustainable and repeatable over time. My personal growth will manifest infinity.

I am a global citizen, a mindful traveler, and a captain of my journey. And I will keep my inner compass pointed at the core of life on this planet, which is love. Love for all people, cultures, creatures, and environments.

Signed: _____

APPENDIX

———

INTRODUCTION

2019 Aviation Benefits Report. Industry High-level Group. Accessed May 5, 2020. https://www.icao.int/sustainability/ Documents/AVIATION-BENEFITS-2019-web.pdf.

Buchanan, Larry, Quoctrung Bui, and Jugal K. Patel. "Black Lives Matter May Be the Largest Movement in US History." New York Times, July 3, 2020. https://www.nytimes.com/interac-tive/2020/07/03/us/george-floyd-protests-crowd-size.html.

Office of the Mayor. Government of the District of Colombia. Accessed June 9, 2020. https://mayor.dc.gov/release/mayor-bowser-renames-portion-16th-street-nw-black-lives-matter-plaza.

Zaru, Deena. "KRS-One gets political: What's fake and what's real in politics?" CNN Politics, August 16, 2017. https://www.cnn.com/2015/11/25/politics/krs-one-election-2016/index.html.

PART I: PREPARING FOR THE JOURNEY

Smolan, Rick. Inside Tracks: Robyn Davidson's Solo Journey Across the Outback. New York: Against All Odds Productions, 2014.

CHAPTER 1

Carbon Footprint. "Flight carbon footprint calculator." Accessed May 5, 2020. https://calculator.carbonfootprint.com/calculator. aspx.

Conservation International. "Carbon Footprint Calculator." Accessed May 5, 2020. https://www.conservation.org/carbon-footprint-calculator#/.

International Civil Aviation Organization. "ICAO Carbon Emissions Calculator." Accessed May 6, 2020. https://www.icao.int/environmental-protection/Carbonoffset/Pages/default.aspx.

Kanbanize. "5 Whys: The Ultimate Root Cause Analysis Tool." Accessed May 10, 2020. https://kanbanize.com/lean-management/improvement/5-whys-analysis-tool.

TerraPass. "Carbon Calculator." Accessed May 6, 2020. https://www.terrapass.com/carbon-footprint-calculator?gclid=C-jwKCAjw-5v7BRAmEiwAJ3DpuGEphJHKgK1_3FncVqKuxV-4vc1TWMVs4EFOA5dHFhmZH_96xjxKMNxoCPSkQAvD_BwE.

US Environmental Protection Agency. "Energy and the Environment: Greenhouse Gas Equivalencies Calculator." Last modified March 2020. https://www.epa.gov/energy/green-house-gas-equivalencies-calculator.

PART II: FINDING TRUTH

MenchTum, Rigoberta. "The Problem of Racism on the Threshold of the 21st Century." Accessed May 5, 2020. https://www.un.org/WCAR/e-kit/indigenous.htm.

CHAPTER 3

Emory University, Center for Digital Scholarship. "Slave Voyages Project." Accessed June 2, 2020. https://www.slavevoyages.org/.

Flahaux, Marie-Laurence, Bruno Schoumaker. "Democratic Republic of the Congo: A Migration History Marked by Crises and Restrictions." Migration Policy Institute, April 20, 2016. https://www.migrationpolicy.org/article/democratic-republic-congo-migration-history-marked-crises-and-restrictions.

Green, Victor. *The Negro Motorist Green-Book: 1940 Facsimile Edition*. New York: Independently published, 1936.

Jewell, K. Sue. From mammy to Miss America and beyond: Cultural images and the shaping of US social policy, 1st Edition. London, United Kingdom: Routledge & CRC Press, 1992.

Llamoca, Janice. "The Secret Revolutionary History of Tupac Shakur's Name," TrackRecord, June 23, 2017. https://track-record.net/the-secret-revolutionary-history-of-tupac-shak-urs-name-1819093454.

Patten, Dominic. "Tupac Shakur Has Tix for Tonight's VP Debate Thanks to Mike Pence in Dig at Kamala Harris Calling Dead Icon Her Favorite Living Rapper." Deadline, October 7, 2020. https://deadline.com/2020/10/tupac-shakur-vp-debate-kamala-harris-mike-pence-campaign-jason-miller-1234593257/.

Reuters Staff. "Fact check: Kamala Harris did not say she listened to Snoop Dogg and Tupac while smoking marijuana in college." Reuters, August 20, 2020. https://www.reuters.com/article/uk-factcheck-kamala-harris-snoop-dogg-tu-idUSKBN25G1IL.

Taylor, Candacy. Overground Railroad: The Green Book and the Roots of Black Travel in America. New York: Abrams Press, 2020.

Walker, Charles. "Berkeley Review of Latin American Studies, Fall 2014, Peru: Reflections of Tupac Amaru." University of California Berkley, Center for Latin American Studies. Last modified October 25, 2018. https://clas.berkeley.edu/research/peru-reflections-tupac-amaru.

White House. "Executive Order on Combating Race and Sex Stereotyping." September 22, 2020. https://www.whitehouse.gov/presidential-actions/executive-order-combating-race-sex-stereotyping/.

CHAPTER 4

Arit, John. "Lupita Nyong'o Ended Kenya and Mexico's Mini-Feud Over Her Nationality," The Atlantic, March 3, 2014. https://www.theatlantic.com/culture/archive/2014/03/lupita-nyongo-ended-kenya-and-mexicos-mini-feud-over-her-national-ity/358766/.

Bianc[...]Bianculli, David. "Comic Hasan Minhaj On Roasting Trump and Growing Up A 'Third Culture Kid." Interview by David Bianculli. Fresh Air, NPR, December 29, 2017. Audio, 37:00. https://www.npr.org/2018/11/02/663389616/comic-hasan-minhaj-on-roasting-trump-and-growing-up-a-third-culture-kid.

Coogler, Ryan, dir. Black Panther. 2018; Burbank, CA: Marvel Studios. 2018.

DHL Global. "DHL Global Connectedness Index." Accessed September 12, 2020. https://www.dhl.com/global-en/home/insights-and-innovation/thought-leadership/case-studies/global-connectedness-index.html.

Garcia-Navarro, Lulu and Sarah Handel. "It Never Existed Before: M.I.A. On Changing Pop and Documenting Her Story." Interview by Lulu Garcia-Navarro. Weekend Edition Sunday, NPR, September 30, 2018. Audio, 7:00. https://www.npr.org/2018/09/30/653021947/it-never-existed-before-m-i-a-on-changing-pop-and-documenting-her-story#:~:text=Live%20Sessions-,'It%20Never%20Existed%20Before'%3A%20M.I.A.,-for%20women%20who%20speak%20out..

History Channel. "Silk Road." A&E Television Networks, LLC., Last modified September 26, 2019. https://www.history.com/topics/ancient-middle-east/silk-road.

Mahajan, Karan. "Stateless." Airbnb Magazine, December/January 2020, 127-137.

Mayberry, Kate. "Third Culture Kids: Citizens of everywhere and nowhere." BBC News. November 18, 2016. https://www.bbc.com/worklife/article/20161117-third-culture-kids-citizens-of-everywhere-and-nowhere.

Munachim, Amah. "Lupita Nyong'o to star in movie adaptation of Trevor Noah's book 'Born A Crime," CNN News. February 22, 2018, CNN World. https://www.cnn.com/2018/02/22/africa/lupita-nyongo-trevor-noah-born-a-crime/index.html.

NASA. "Greetings to the Universe in 55 Different Languages." Accessed May 5, 2020. https://voyager.jpl.nasa.gov/golden-record/whats-on-the-record/greetings/.

National Geographic. "Globalization." National Geographic, Encyclopedia, Resource Library. Accessed September 20, 2020. https://www.nationalgeographic.org/encyclopedia/globalization/.

Peterson, Roman. "Hope and Humor." *TimeforKids*. April 9, 2019. https://www.timeforkids.com/G56/hope-humor-trevor-noah/.

Singh, Lilly. How to Be a Bawse: A Guide to Conquering Life. New York: Ballantine Books, 2017.

TCK World: The Official Home of Third Culture Kids. "TCK World proudly presents: Dr. Ruth Hill Useem—the sociologist/anthropologist who first coined the term "Third Culture Kid" (TCK)." Accessed August 20, 2020. http://www.tckworld.com/useem/home.html.

United Nations Children's Fund. "Lilly Singh." UNICEF People. Accessed September 12, 2020. https://www.unicef.org/people/people_96639.html.

White House. "Executive Order Protecting the Nation from Foreign Terrorist Entry into the United States." January 27, 2017. https://www.whitehouse.gov/presidential-actions/executive-order-protecting-nation-foreign-terrorist-entry-united-states/.

Yam, Kimberly. "Lilly Singh Puts 'Superwoman' Name to Rest In Emotional Instagram Post." HuffPost, Entertainment, Verizon Media. Last modified August 15, 2019. https://www.huffpost.com/entry/lilly-singh-superwoman-name-ends_n_5d54b-9b7e4b056fafd073a59.

CHAPTER 5

Gardner, Chris. "Biography." Chris Gardner's official website. Accessed June 4, 2020. https://www.chrisgardnermedia.com/biography.

Green, Kelly. "What I Learnt Forest Bathing." Eco-Age, May 15, 2019. https://eco-age.com/magazine/what-i-learnt-forest-bathing/#:~:text=Forest%20bathing%20has%20many%20wellbe-ing,sense%20of%20calm%20and%20relaxation.

National Park Service. "The Restless Giant." National Park Service, Yellowstone. Accessed June 4, 2020. https://www.nps.gov/yell/index.htm.

Perko, Tomislav. "How to travel the world with almost no money." Filmed February 2015 at TEDxTUHH, Hamburg University of Technology, Hamburg, Germany. Video, 18:18. https://www.youtube.com/watch?v=R7vmHGAshi8&list=PLsoP5g-mr6J1UUJUpLb33MVwMyl8Q5Hnc8&index=3&t=0s&app=desktop.

Pursuit of Happiness, Inc. "Abraham Maslow." Accessed June 5, 2020. https://www.pursuit-of-happiness.org/history-of-happiness/abraham-maslow/?gclid=CjoKCQiA7qP9BRCLARIsABDaZzi-yJbpPAT3RsQvWYTouwEDkyXdNDMxC2yNhZOVe-LH75v-vZ-Km8m38aArPBEALw_wcB.

Schlichter, Sarah. "The Art of Slow Travel." Smarter Travel (blog). February 12, 2019. https://www.smartertravel.com/art-slow-travel/.

Sherman, Jeremy. "Face-it Versus Escapist Coping Strategies." Psychology Today, April 10, 2017. https://www.psychologytoday.com/us/blog/ambigamy/201704/face-it-versus-escapist-coping-strategies#:~:text=Face%2Dit%20strategies%20supply%20us,easy%20to%20ignore%20our%20reality.

Strayed, Cheryl. Wild: From Lost to Found on the Pacific Crest Trail. New York: Alfred A. Knopf, 2012.

Taibi, Selima, dir. Expedition Happiness. Written by Selima Taibi and Felix Starck. Aired May 4, 2017, on Netflix.

CHAPTER 6

Berardelli, Jeff. "How climate change is making hurricanes more dangerous," Yale Climate Connections, accessed May 5, 2020. https://yaleclimateconnections.org/2019/07/how-climate-change-is-making-hurricanes-more-dangerous/?gclid=EAIaIQobChMI5Mn3p-aU6gIVg43ICh3tK-wOlEAAYASAAEgLX6vD_BwE.

Emmerich, Roland, dir. Day After Tomorrow. 2004; Los Angeles, CA: 20th Century Studios, Inc. 2004.

Encyclopedia Britannica Online. Academic ed. s.v. "Taino." Accessed May 5, 2020, https://www.britannica.com/topic/Taino.

NASA. "Understanding Sea Level," NASA. Accessed May 5, 2020. https://sealevel.nasa.gov/understanding-sea-level/global-sea-level/ice-melt.

New York Center for Puerto Rican Studies. Puerto Rico One Year After Hurricane Maria. The City University of New York. October 2018.

Thunberg, Greta. "Greta Thunberg blasts world leaders: We will never forgive you." CBC News. Streamed live on September 23, 2019. YouTube video, 4:28. https://www.youtube.com/watch?v=h3SmqCcNbU8.

CHAPTER 7

Chang, Jeff. "It's a Hip-Hop World." Foreign Policy, The Slate Group, October 12, 2009. https://foreignpolicy.com/2009/10/12/its-a-hip-hop-world/.

Khatih, Joumana. "What Anthony Bourdain Meant to People of Color." New York Times, June 12, 2018. https://www.nytimes.com/2018/06/12/dining/anthony-bourdain-ethnic-communities.html.

The Center for Nonviolent Communication. "What is Nonviolent Communication." Accessed May 5, 2020. https://www.cnvc.org/learn-nvc/what-is-nvc.

Rory, PQ. "Hip Hop History: From the Streets to the Mainstream." Icon Music Blog. Last modified November 25, 2019. https://iconcollective.edu/hip-hop-history/.

Tewodros Workneh and H. Leslie Steeves, "Anthony Bourdain: Parts Unknown in Africa: Cultural Brokerage, "Going Native," and Colonial Nostalgia," International Journal of Communication, 13(2019).

Young, Scott Young, Ultralearning. New York: HarperCollins Publishers, 2019.

CHAPTER 8

Avery, Jen. "The Ultimate List of Sharing Economy Services for Travel." Thrifty Nomads (blog). February 4, 2016. https://thriftynomads.com/the-ultimate-sharing-economy-list-worldwide-travel/.

Bridges, Khiara M. "How Racial Hierarchy Kills," Time, June 2020, 44.

Budget Travel Babes. "Is Couchsurfing safe? How to use Couchsurfing as a solo female traveler." Budget Travel Babes, July 1, 2020. https://www.budgettravelbabes.com/couchsurfing/.

Chi, Clifford. "What Is a Digital Nomad and How Do You Become One?" HubSpot blog. Accessed September 5, 2020. https://blog.hubspot.com/marketing/digital-nomad.

Encyclopaedia Britannica Online. Academic ed. s.v. "Inner Mongolia." Accessed September 3, 2020. https://www.britannica.com/place/Inner-Mongolia.

Merriam-Webster. s.v. "nomad (n.)." *Accessed September 3, 2020.* https://www.merriam-webster.com/dictionary/nomad.

PART IV: RESILIENCE
Smolan, Rick. Inside Tracks: Robyn Davidson's Solo Journey Across the Outback. New York: Against All Odds Productions, 2014.

CHAPTER 9
Flanagan, Mike, dir. Haunting of Bly Manor. Written by Mike Flanagan. Aired October 9, 2020, on Netflix.

Taibi, Selima, dir. Expedition Happiness. Written by Selima Taibi and Felix Starck. Aired May 4, 2017, on Netflix.

Nomadic Matt. "14 Ways to Safely Hitchhike Across the United States." Nomadic Matt's Travel Site. Last modified August 18, 2018. https://www.nomadicmatt.com/travel-blogs/hitchhike-across-united-states/.

Perko, Tomislav. "How to travel the world with almost no money." Filmed February 2015 at TEDxTUHH, Hamburg University of Technology, Hamburg, Germany. Video, 18:18. https://www.youtube.com/watch?v=R7vmHGAshi8&list=PLsoP5g-mr6J1UUJUpLb33MVwMyl8Q5Hnc8&index=3&t=0s&app=desktop.

Veitch, Adam. June 14, 2019. "Comuna 13: How a Medellin community turned a war zone into a tourist attraction." Colombia Reports.

CHAPTER 10

Aschwanden, Christie. "How 'Superspreading' Events Drive Most COVID-19 Spread." *Scientific American,* June 23, 2020.

Boyd, Connor. "Globe-trotting Vietnamese daughter of a steel magnate 'infected SEVEN Britons who shared a plane with her with coronavirus' after attending Gucci and Saint Laurent fashion shows in Milan and Paris." *Daily Mail,* March 11, 2020. https://www.dailymail.co.uk/health/article-8082803/Seven-Brits-test-positive-coronavirus-Vietnam-plane-globe-trotting-super-spreader.html.

Jordan, Adrienne. "How COVID-19 Is Changing The Game For Travel Influencers." Forbes Travel, June 9, 2020. https://www.

forbes.com/sites/forbes-personal-shopper/2020/10/30/todd-snyder-ll-bean-collection-from-away-2020/?sh=73652ee43c59.

Max, D.T. "The Public-Shaming Pandemic." New Yorker, September 21, 2020. https://www.newyorker.com/magazine/2020/09/28/the-public-shaming-pandemic.

Soderbergh, Steven, dir. Contagion. 2011; Los Angeles, CA: Warner Bros. Studio. 2011.

Weiner, Eric. "Travel Has Changed—So Must We." AFAR Magazine, September 17, 2020. https://www.afar.com/magazine/five-ways-to-travel-more-responsibly?utm_source=Sailthru&utm_medium=email&utm_campaign=091820%20State-Parks&utm_content=Final&utm_term=Daily%20Wander%20%28Have%20opened%20newsletter%20before%29.

PART V: GIVING BACK

Stanford University. "Gandhi, Mohandas." Martin Luther King, Jr. Encyclopedia. The Martin Luther King, Jr. Research and Education Institute. Accessed September 6, 2020. https://kinginstitute.stanford.edu/.

CHAPTER 11

Bergmann, Manuel. "About Me." Coachingforcause. Accessed on September 5, 2020. https://coachingforcause.com/.

Bergmann Manuel. "How to Cultivate Environmental Wellness and Zero Waste Living with Manuel Bergmann." Joy Energy Time, May 31, 2019. Audio, 53:00. https://www.joyenergytime.com/

ep-080-how-to-cultivate-environmental-wellness-and-ze-
ro-waste-living-with-manuel-bergmann-interview/.

Chan, Melissa. "The Price of Protest." Time, Double Issue. September 21 and 28, 2020.

Frayer, Lauren. Black Lives Matter Gets Indians Talking About
Skin Lightening And Colorism." NPR, July 9, 2020. https://
www.npr.org/sections/goatsandsoda/2020/07/09/860912124/
black-lives-matter-gets-indians-talking-about-skin-lighten-
ing-and-colorism.

King, Martin Luther. "My Pilgrimage to Nonviolence." Fellowship,
September 1958, 4–9. The Papers of Martin Luther King, Jr.
Volume IV: Symbol of the Movement, January 1957-December
1958, Editors, Clayborne Carson, Susan Carson, Adrienne Clay,
Virginia Shadron, and Kieran Taylor. University of California
Press at Berkeley and Los Angeles, 2000. https://kinginstitute.
stanford.edu/king-papers/documents/my-pilgrimage-nonvi-
olence.

King, Yolanda Renee. "Yolanda Renee King, MLK's granddaughter: Enough is enough," CBS News. Streamed live on March
24, 2018. YouTube video, 1:57. https://www.youtube.com/
watch?v=TvskFQN-4eY.

Stanford University. "Gandhi, Mohandas." Martin Luther King,
Jr. Encyclopedia. The Martin Luther King, Jr. Research and
Education Institute. Accessed September 6, 2020. https://
kinginstitute.stanford.edu/.

Thunberg, Greta. "Greta Thunberg blasts world leaders: We will never forgive you." CBC News. Streamed live on September 23, 2019. YouTube video, 4:28. https://www.youtube.com/watch?v=h3SmqCcNbU8.

Weibel, Peter. Global activism: Art & Conflict in the 21st Century. Massachusetts: The MIT Press, 2015.

Greta Thunberg, "Greta Thunberg blasts world leaders: We will never forgive you," CBC News, streamed live on September 23, 2019, YouTube video, 4:28.

CHAPTER 12

2019 Aviation Benefits Report. Industry High-level Group. Accessed on May 5, 2020 from https://www.icao.int/sustainability/Documents/AVIATION-BENEFITS-2019-web.pdf.

Aksharavani. "Stories from the Site," Aksharavani, An Adaptive Community School in Hyderabad, India. Accessed September 5, 2020. https://aksharavani.wordpress.com/community-stories/.

BookBrowse LLC. "BookBrowse's Favorite Quotes." Accessed September 22, 2020. https://www.bookbrowse.com/quotes/detail/index.cfm/quote_number/379/never-doubt-that-a-small-group-of-thoughtful-committed-people-can-change-the-world.

Diakite, Parker. "Ghana Launches 'Beyond The Return' Campaign." Travel Noire, January 5, 2020. https://travelnoire.com/ghana-beyond-the-return-campaign.

Diakite, Parker. "How Ghana's Year of Return Campaign Put Black Destinations In The Spotlight." Travel Noire, April 28, 2020. https://travelnoire.com/ghana-year-return-campaign-black-destinations-in-the-spotlight.

Engler, Sarah. "30 Ways to Travel with a Lighter Footprint." Airbnb Magazine. Accessed May 5, 2020. https://medium.com/airbnbmag/30-ways-to-travel-with-a-lighter-footprint-645349a28345.

Ethical Influencers. "Josephine of Treesnpeace." Accessed September 20, 2020. https://ethicalinfluencers.co.uk/josephine-treesnpeace/.

Global Citizen. "Citizenship." Accessed September 20, 2020. www.globalcitizen.org.

Olmer, Naya and Dan Rutherford. "US domestic airline fuel efficiency ranking, 2015–2016." The International Council on Clean Transportation. December 14, 2017. https://theicct.org/publications/us-domestic-airline-fuel-efficiency-ranking-2015-16.

Reality Check Team. "African diaspora: Did Ghana's Year of Return attract foreign visitors?" BBC News. January 30, 2020. https://www.bbc.com/news/world-africa-51191409.

Reid, Thomas. "Essays on the intellectual powers of man." Dublin, Printed for L. White, 1786. Accessed September 20, 2020. www.openlibrary.org.

Thunberg, Greta. "Greta Thunberg blasts world leaders: We will never forgive you." CBC News. Streamed live on September 23, 2019. YouTube video, 4:28. https://www.youtube.com/watch?v=h3SmqCcNbU8.

United Nations Educational, Scientific, and Cultural Organization. "Priorities." Accessed September 20, 2020. http://www.unesco.org/new/en/gefi/priorities/.

US Environmental Protection Agency. "Energy and the Environment: Greenhouse Gas Equivalencies Calculator." Last modified March 2020. https://www.epa.gov/energy/greenhouse-gas-equivalencies-calculator.

Weiner, Eric. "Travel Has Changed—So Must We." *AFAR Magazine*. September 17, 2020. https://www.afar.com/magazine/five-ways-to-travel-more-responsibly?utm_source=Sailthru&utm_medium=email&utm_campaign=091820%20StateParks&utm_content=Final&utm_term=Daily%20Wander%20%28Have%20opened%20newsletter%20before%29.

CHAPTER 13

Baskas, Harriet. "Nine Travel Tips from Astronauts," *Smithsonian Magazine*, August 9, 2018. https://www.smithsonianmag.com/travel/nine-travel-tips-astronauts-have-taken-space-earth-180969959/#:~:text=%E2%80%9CUse%20a%20checklist%2C%E2%80%9D%20advises,to%20every%20time%20I%20travel.%E2%80%9D.

Gibbons, Chris. "What do Smart Cities have to do with Interoperability?" December 13, 2019. Accessed from https://hub.nic-us.

org/events/what-do-smart-cities-have-to-do-with-interoperability

Health Information and Management Systems Society. "HIMSS Webinar: Smart Communities & Cities - cases from Finland." January 21, 2020. https://healthcapitalhelsinki.fi/himss-webinar/.

Klimek, Chris. "With the New Movie Ad Astra, James Gray and Brad Pitt Offer a "Plausible" Vision of Late-21st Century Space Travel." Air & Space Magazine, Smithsonian Institution, September 20, 2019. https://www.airspacemag.com/airspacemag/new-movie-emad-astraem-writer-director-james-gray-and-producerstar-brad-pitt-offer-plausible-vision-late-21st-century-space-travel-180973168/.

Lemire, Jonathan and Zeke Miller. "Biden wins White House, vowing new direction for divided US." Associated Press, November 7, 2020. https://apnews.com/article/Biden-Trump-US-election-2020-results-fd58df73aa677acb74fce2a69adb71f9.

NASA. "Current Space Act Agreements." NASA. Last modified October 5, 2020. https://www.nasa.gov/partnerships/about.html.

NASA. "NASA Astronauts Launch from America in Historic Test Flight of SpaceX Crew Dragon." NASA, May 30, 2020. https://www.nasa.gov/press-release/nasa-astronauts-launch-from-america-in-historic-test-flight-of-spacex-crew-dragon.

Shanghai Highlights. "China Train Types." Accessed September 3, 2020. https://www.shanghaihighlights.com/shanghai-train-schedule/china-train-types.htm

CHAPTER 14

Encyclopaedia Britannica Online. s.v. "pledge." Accessed September 3, 2020. https://www.britannica.com/search?query=pledge.

Leave No Trace Center for Outdoor Ethics. "The Seven Principles." Accessed September 5, 2020. https://lnt.org/why/7-principles/.

Williams, Shirley. "The Black Child's Pledge." HERB: Resources for Teachers. Accessed June 22, 2020. https://herb.ashp.cuny.edu/items/show/1254.

ACKNOWLEDGMENTS

———

First, I must start with Eric Koester. From the very beginning, you have been integral to my completion of this book through your year-long book program and countless Zoom calls.

I'd like to also thank the incredible work of my editorial team as we selected my most impactful stories. I couldn't have asked for a better publishing company to help me spread good into the world.

Thank you to New Degree Press, Creators Institute, my 2020 author cohort, and the countless talented individuals I met through this book journey. You all taught me so much about the world of writing and storytelling. When I was four years old and answered the question of what I wanted to be when I grew up, I said author. Thanks to everyone below, that has become a reality. As part of this journey, I encourage each of you to spread the word.

Publishing Team

Brian Bies	Pea Richelle White	Robert Alston
Gjorgji Pejkovski	Kristy Elam	Alexander Pavlovich
Linda Berardelli	Stefan Mancevski	Amanda Brown
Sherman Morrison	Leila Summers	Liana Moisescu
Mackenzie Finklea	Chanda Elaine Spurlock	Kyra Ann Dawkins

To my International Beta Reader Community. Your contributions and faith inspired me to keep writing amid one of the most difficult and game-changing times of our lives.

There are several Super-Beta readers I'd like to recognize for the extra love you showed the book and myself during the process. I appreciate the long conversations and interviews, the feedback on early versions of this book, the many audio messages we exchanged, the articles you tagged me in, and your overall support of my message to the world.

Susanna Surio	Nicholas D'Souza	Anjana Sreedhar
Davin Surio	Elizabeth Ivanecky	Master O'Neal
Girish Surio	Moises Zamora	Danielle Douglin
Zoltan Kiraly	Janet Oputa	Lemar Griffin
Austin Nieves	Carole Greenwell	DaQuawn Bruce

Rebecca DeJesus-Wagoner

Christina Powell

Linn Haglund

Meron Begashaw

Anusha Koduru

Tequam Tiruneh

Ndaya Cynthia

Kennedy Ezumah

Victor Folayan

Jeremie Gluckman-Picard

Kelsey Rumburg

Robert W. Orttung

International Beta Reader Community

Lydia Daniels

Pamela Ascon

Natasha Chakraborty

Zeeshawn Chughtai

Hillary Peabody

Shereef Elnahal

Mahli Knutson

Sarvani Singh

Zacher Bayonne

Pavithira Vasudevan

Michael Bonney

Shobha Dasari

Sheran Vasudevan

Gregory M Jacobson

Nelli Ghazaryan

Mackenzie Copley

Shawn Wilkins

Hersila Patel

Anastasia Tarmann

Niche Alder

Tyler Lederer

Apryl Perry

Sandy Lee

Ram Ramachandran

Michael Hannan

Megan Shaheen

MaryAnn Cooney

Rebecca O'Neal

Damilola Adeyemo

Brenda Thomas

Mario Cummings

Deanna Amodeo

Corey Joyner

Jessica Lay

Candice Schottenloher

Pierre Vigilance

Michael Fraser	Meron Begashaw	Marlon Austin
Candice C Rambarath	Shirin Porkar	Aika Aluc
Charlie Bolling	Haley Newlin	Cara J Person
Alexander & Laura Vazquez	Ellen Pliska	John Lane
Alice Mathew	Damika Barr	Emma Hawkes
Jerome Paul	Chanel Rutland	Victoria Pless
Kerrianne Hopkins	Deidre Blackmore	Melissa Cianci
Karl Ensign	Valerie Rogers	Shalisha Grace Maddela
Saleema Vellani	Alex Kearly	Ala'a Rafati
Kennedy Ezumah	Alex Dulin	Emily Lapayowker
Jeffrey Ekoma	Kristin Sullivan	Ka Ng
Pallavi Pal	Terrell Baptiste	Chiamaka Ofulue
Mary Terzian	Kaitlyn Allen	Eskedar Hailu Dejene
Priyanka Debnath	Gayatri Sanku	Mahesh Suravarapu
Nikita Gurudas	Carol Yee	Nibras Chowdhury
Thomas Novak	Russ Green	Ankur Jain
Desaray Smith	Rahul Dubey	Sharon V Williams
Tiffany Mosher	Tamar Haddad	